Great Sentences for Great Paragraphs

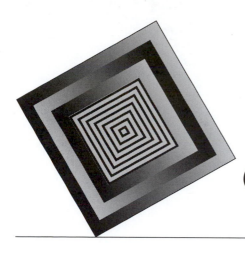

Great Sentences for Great Paragraphs

An Introduction to
Basic Sentences and Paragraphs

Second Edition

Keith S. Folse
University of Central Florida

April Muchmore-Vokoun
Hillsborough Community College

Elena Vestri Solomon
Hillsborough Community College

Houghton Mifflin Company
Boston New York

Publisher: Patricia A. Coryell
Director of ESL Publishing: Susan Maguire
Senior Development Editor: Kathy Sands-Boehmer
Development Editor: BJ Wells
Editorial Assistant: Evangeline Bermas
Senior Project Editor: Tracy Patruno
Senior Manufacturing Coordinator: Priscilla Bailey
Marketing Manager: Annamarie Rice

Cover image: © Dan Yaccarino/The Stock Illustration Source

Printed in the U.S.A.

Library of Congress Control Number: 2003115596

ISBN: 0-618-44416-5

123456789-DBH-08 07 06 05 04

Contents

Unit 7 Writing Sentences with Adjective Clauses and Place Phrases   160

Unit 8 More Practice with Sentences and Paragraphs   182

Appendixes 206

Index   271

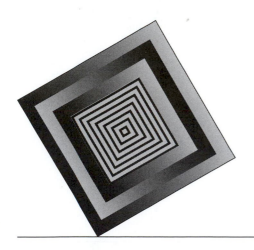

Overview

Great Sentences for Great Paragraphs is the lower-level book of the *Great Paragraphs* and *Great Essays* series of composition books. In *Great Sentences*, students become better writers by focusing their attention on the elements of writing a good sentence within simple paragraphs. This book provides practice that helps students not only to understand the writing process but also to produce a correctly written final product.

The book is designed for students who are novice writers. It is especially suited for beginning to lower intermediate students but may be used with any level writer who is unfamiliar with the basics of writing correct sentences in simple paragraphs. Depending on the class level and the amount of writing that is done outside of class, there is enough material for 60 to 80 classroom hours. If more of the writing is done outside of class, the number of hours for a faster group can be as few as 40.

Great Sentences contains 163 activities with at least 70 suggestions for additional writing. In addition, the appendixes contain supplementary instruction and practices in a wide variety of writing components, including capitalization, spelling rules, articles, prepositions, commas, and adjectives. Of special interest to teachers are Appendix 16, which contains activities to improve students' sentence combination skills, and Appendix 17, which contains extra writing activities for students who need additional help or practice.

A very important feature of *Great Sentences for Great Paragraphs* is the inclusion of 78 sample paragraphs distributed throughout the units. Instead of exercises consisting of unrelated sentences, most of the activities in this book present whole paragraphs of related sentences on a single topic. In addition to providing relevant practice on some aspect of the sentence, these contextualized activities provide learners with more input in English composition and in paragraph organization and cohesion.

For many ESL students, not being able to write effectively and easily in English is a major obstacle to their future educational plans. Thus, the quality of any written work is important. To this end, the activities in this book deal with different elements that can affect the quality of a written product, including grammar, punctuation, and capitalization.

Some ESL students are already good writers in their native language, but others need work in the basic steps involved in the process of composing sentences and paragraphs. These students in particular will benefit from the step-by-step activities in *Great Sentences*.

The teacher is always the best judge of which units and which activities should be covered with any group of students. It is up to you to gauge the needs of your students and then match those needs with the material in this book.

TEXT ORGANIZATION

UNITS 1–8

Great Sentences consists of eight units. Unit 1 and Units 3 through 7 deal with a particular aspect of writing correct sentences in simple paragraphs. Unit 2 introduces students to the basic elements of a paragraph and asks students to analyze these elements. Unit 8 contains an additional 25 writing activities.

In Unit 1, students learn the basic parts of a sentence. Students learn the importance of subjects and verbs in a sentence.

In Unit 2, students see the connection between sentences and paragraphs. Novice writers learn the basic parts of a paragraph and how their sentences can fit into these parts.

In Unit 3, students write about the present. They practice writing sentences using the simple present tense.

In Unit 4, students write about the past. Here students practice the simple past tense of both regular and irregular verbs.

In Unit 5, students practice describing actions. The writing activities in this unit guide students through the use of the present progressive (continuous) tense to accomplish this.

In Unit 6, students write about the future. They have numerous opportunities to use *will* and *be + going to* in their writing and to compare this to the tenses that they have learned in previous units of this book.

Unit 7 offers a more difficult but necessary lesson in writing. Here students learn to build better sentences by using adjective clauses in their writing. Students learn not only the structure of these clauses but also their correct placement within sentences.

Unit 8 consists of 25 activities that provide further guided and free practice of the techniques presented in this text. These activities may be done toward the end of the course, or they may be done while the students are still working in the first seven units of the book. In addition, these activities may be used as remedial help for weaker students or for bonus work for students who have already finished the work in the first seven units.

APPENDIXES

Great Sentences contains 18 appendixes. Appendixes 1 through 15 offer instruction in a wide array of basic writing areas, including a verb tense overview, capitalization, spelling rules for adding *-ed*, irregular past tense, spelling rules for adding *-ing*, stative verbs, the definite article *the*, noncount nouns, possessive adjectives, quantifiers, prepositions, comma rules, order of adjectives, connectors, and definitions of useful language terms. The material is presented in a very simple and clear manner and is accompanied by pertinent examples.

Appendix 16, new to the second edition, is dedicated to sentence writing skills. Individual sentences, taken from the sample paragraphs and activities in each unit, have been isolated and divided into short, choppy sentences that students are asked to combine into longer sentences. This type of activity exercises students' skills in using prepositional phrases, coordinating conjunctions, conjunctive adverbs, and other transitional devices to write concise sentences. After completing the exercises, students are able to check their written products with the original sentences found in the units.

Appendix 17 is a collection of ten guided paragraph activities. Many of these activities require students to read and study short paragraphs, make a series of basic changes, and then rewrite their new paragraph. Other activities are more open-ended. These activities are designed to be done as additional work to support or supplement the material within the main units of the book.

Appendix 18 consists of the peer editing sheets for the peer editing activity in each unit. While we believe that the best way to learn to edit is to practice editing, we believe that lower-level students in particular should not edit written work without the kind of guidance (i.e., teaching) that is provided by these peer editing sheets.

The Answer Key and additional practices for *Great Sentences for Great Paragraphs* can be found at http://esl.college.hmco.com/instructors.

CONTENTS OF A UNIT

Though each unit has a specific writing goal and Grammar and Sentence Structure, the following features appear in almost every unit.

GRAMMAR AND SENTENCE STRUCTURE

One of the biggest problems for many beginning (and even advanced) writers is grammar. While nonnative speakers will always make some errors, it is important to help students realize what their major grammar and sentence structure problems are and then to provide appropriate instruction and practice exercises and activities.

The grammar and sentence structure points are language structures that are necessary to complete the writing tasks within that unit. For example, in Unit 5, Describing Actions, students are asked to pay particular attention to the use of verbs in the present progressive (continuous) tense because this language structure is necessary to write descriptions of actions. Likewise, in Unit 7, students are taught to build up sentence variety through the use of adjective clauses. Students first learn about adjective clauses but are then asked to produce sentences and then small paragraphs that incorporate this sentence structure.

SENTENCE DEVELOPMENT

One of the main goals of *Great Sentences* is for students to learn the basics of the simple sentence in English. However, an equally important and related goal is for students to move beyond the simple sentence and begin including compound and complex sentences in their original writing. Thus, this section provides important practice in helping students expand their repertoire of sentence structures in English.

WRITER'S NOTES

Rather than large boxed areas overflowing with information, *Great Sentences* features small chunks of writing advice under this heading. The content of these writer's notes varies from brainstorming techniques, peer editing guidelines, and journal writing advice to using commas correctly.

BUILDING BETTER SENTENCES

After every Word Building exercise, students are asked to turn to Appendix 16 and work on building better sentences. This activity focuses on students' sentence-level writing skills. For those students who lack confidence in producing longer or more complicated sentences, this type of activity concentrates on the manipulation of words and ideas at the sentence level.

WORD BUILDING

In every unit before the original writing practice, students study affixes and parts of speech in the Word Building activity. In these activities, vocabulary words have been taken from each unit's writing, and special attention is paid to the affixes that are used, their meanings, and their usage in a grammatical sentence. Understanding how affixes are related to the different parts of speech allows students to expand their understanding of word formation in English, giving them a broader vocabulary base and a better understanding of word order for better writing skills.

EDITING

Teaching students to edit their own writing is one of the most important goals of any writing course. To this end, *Great Sentences* provides several types of editing practice and activities throughout the units.

GUIDED WRITING PRACTICE

Because of the lower proficiency of students using this book, guided writing practice activities are included. In the more basic exercises, students are asked to copy a paragraph and make only four or five rather simple changes. Eventually, the changes become more complicated. While the students are not writing original work here, they are gaining critical confidence with the conventions of good writing, such as the use of capital letters, indenting, handwriting (or typing), and punctuation.

PEER EDITING

Each unit contains an activity in which a student swaps papers with another student and then makes comments about the partner's paper. Because of the lower proficiency level of the students, it is especially important to provide novice writers and editors with detailed guidelines about what to look for when editing or reviewing someone's work. Unit 1 explains what to keep in mind when reviewing someone else's work.

JOURNAL WRITING

One of the best ways to learn to write is by writing. Journal writing offers a happy compromise between informal letter (or e-mail) writing to friends and formal paragraph or essay writing. Journal writing encourages students to write about topics that they are interested in. To this end, each unit has a list of ten possible journal topics with a series of questions to encourage original student writing. These topics may be developed into class assignments, but since students' purposes for learning to write in English can vary so much, we leave the topics and parameters for course writing up to the individual instructor.

ABOUT THE ACTIVITIES AND PRACTICES

Teachers have long noticed that although students do well with grammar in discrete sentences, they may have problems with the same grammar when it occurs in a paragraph. Because of this, most of the activities and practices in *Great Sentences for Great Paragraphs* work with complete paragraphs. Thus, instead of five unrelated sentences for practice with the past tense, we offer a paragraph of five sentences. Our hope is that by practicing the grammatical structure within the target medium, students will produce more accurate writing sooner. The large number of such paragraphs (78) allows a great deal of freedom on the teacher's part in planning this course.

The earliest ESL composition textbooks were merely extensions of ESL grammar classes. The activities in these books did not practice English composition as much as they did ESL grammar points. Later books, on the other hand, tended to focus too much on the composing process. We feel that this focus ignores the important fact that the real goal for our ESL students is both to produce a presentable product and to understand the composing practice. From our years of ESL and other L2 teaching experience, we believe that *Great Sentences for Great Paragraphs* allows students to achieve this goal.

On the Web

For the answer key, additional exercises, and other instuctor resources, visit the *Great Sentences* instructor website at

http://esl.college.hmco.com/instructors

Additional exercises for each unit are available to students on the *Great Sentences* student website at

http://esl.college.hmco.com/students

ACKNOWLEDGMENTS

We would like to thank ESL and English composition colleagues who generously shared their ideas, insights, and feedback on L2 writing, community college and university English course requirements, and textbook design. In addition, we would like to thank teachers on two electronic lists, TESL-L and TESLIE-L, who responded to our original queries and thereby helped us write this book.

We offer special thanks to our incredible editors at Houghton Mifflin. Susan Maguire has been a constant source of guidance and inspiration throughout the completion of not only *Great Sentences* but also *Great Paragraphs* and *Great Essays*. Likewise, we are indebted to Kathy Sands Boehmer, who offered us ideas and feedback and helped us keep us and this writing project on schedule. In addition, we would like to thank our development editor, BJ Wells of Modesto Junior College, for her valuable insights and help during the editing of the Second Edition.

We would also like to thank the following reviewers who offered ideas and suggestions that shaped our revisions:

Richard Appelbaum, Broward Community College

Jane Shea, Quinsagamond Community College

Beth Snyder, Bergen Community College

Elizabeth Wagenheim, Prince George's Community College

Finally, many thanks go to our students, who have taught us what composition ought to be, and to the numerous teachers who have given us such positive feedback on our earlier works, *Great Paragraphs* and *Great Essays*. Without these people, this work would most certainly have been impossible.

Keith S. Folse
April Muchmore-Vokoun
Elena Vestri Solomon

Understanding Sentence Basics

GOAL: To learn how to write a correct simple sentence

SENTENCE DEVELOPMENT: Simple sentences

GRAMMAR AND SENTENCE STRUCTURE: Subjects, verbs, and objects; the verb *be*

WHAT IS A SENTENCE?

A sentence is a group of words that expresses a complete thought. The words in a sentence are in a special order. Examples of sentences are *Joe likes basketball.* and *The weather is cold today.*

Do You Know?

The sentences on the left are English. The sentences on the right are not English. Do you know what language they are? Try to guess the languages, and then check your answers on the bottom of page 37.

The class has twelve students.	Ci sono dodici studenti nella classe.
The student is from Canada.	這位學生是來自加拿大。
Mike speaks French and English.	Miklós beszél franciául és angolul.
A cat has a tail and four legs.	Pisica are o coadă și patru picioare.

1

Words, sentences, paragraphs, and essays are all related. Words can go together to make sentences. Sentences can go together to make a paragraph. Finally, paragraphs can be combined into an essay. In this book, you will study sentences. Then you will study sentences in paragraphs.

Connections

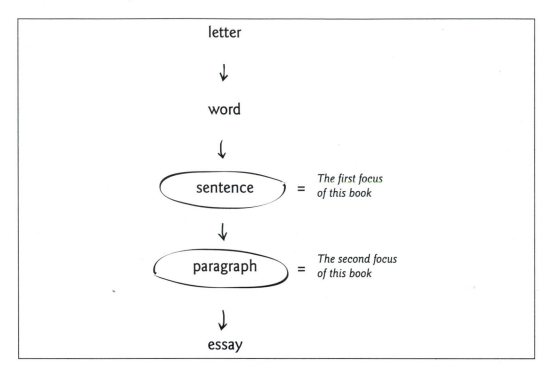

Activity 1 **Words into Sentences**

The sentences below are not correct. The words are in the wrong order. Write the words in the correct order to make correct English sentences. The first one has been done for you.

Topic: Write about your family.

1. is not / very big / My family / .   *My family is not very big.*

2. only four people / There are / .   _____

3. I / two parents / have / .   _____

4. José / my father's name / is / .   _____

5. My mother's name / Karina / is / .   _____

6. have / I / one brother / .   _____

7. His name / Andy / is / .   _____

8. very much / I / my family / love / .   _____

| Activity 2 | Writing Simple Sentences: A Diagnostic |

Write five to eight sentences about your family. Follow the examples in Activity 1.

Topic: Write about your family.

1. _____

2. _____

3. _____

4. _____

5. _____

6. _____

7. _____

8. _____

WORKING WITH SENTENCES

In this section you will learn the basics of how to write simple sentences, including capitalization and some punctuation rules.

WRITER'S NOTE: Begin a Sentence with a Capital Letter

In English, there are two kinds of letters: capital letters (H, R) and small letters (h, r). Most of the time we use small letters. However, we always begin a sentence with a capital letter.

Incorrect:	the boxes on the table are heavy.
Correct:	**T**he boxes on the table are heavy.
Incorrect:	where do you live?
Correct:	**W**here do you live?

Look back at any five sentences in the unit so far. Can you find any sentences that do not begin with a capital letter? (The answer is "no"!)

(NOTE: See Appendix 3 for capitalization rules.)

In English, there are three ways to end a sentence:

- with a period (.)
- with a question mark (?)
- with an exclamation point (!)

WRITER'S NOTE: End a Sentence with a Period

The most common or usual way to end a sentence is with a period. A sentence that tells us information is called a statement. We usually put a period at the end of a sentence that is a statement. For example, this sentence has a period at the end. Can you find any sentences in this unit that do not end with a period? (The answer is "yes"!)

Incorrect:	Brazil is a large country
Correct:	Brazil is a large country.
Incorrect:	I don't like coffee with sugar
Correct:	I don't like coffee with sugar.

Activity 3   **Unscrambling and Writing Sentences**

Unscramble the groups of words on the next page to write simple sentences. Be sure to begin each sentence with a capital letter. In addition, be sure to put a period at the end of sentences.

Topic: Write about something good to eat.

1. spaghetti / most kids / like

   _____

2. enjoy / they / the taste of spaghetti

   _____

3. the smell of spaghetti / they / love

   _____

4. tomato sauce / on their spaghetti / some kids / put

   _____

5. like / on their spaghetti / cheese / other kids

   _____

6. is very / most kids / popular with / spaghetti

   _____

Activity 4	**Writing Simple Sentences**

Copy the sentences you unscrambled in Activity 3. In every sentence, change the word spaghetti *to* ice cream. *Make other appropriate changes as necessary.*

1. _____

2. _____

3. _____

4. _____

5. _____

6. _____

Editing

Activity 5 — **Editing Simple Sentences**

Read this list of eight sentences about a taxi driver. In each sentence, correct the capitalization mistakes and add a period at the end. Then write the sentences on another piece of paper. The first one has been done for you.

Topic: Write about a person and his or her job.

    M

1. ~~m~~y cousin Albert has an interesting job.

2. albert is a taxi driver

3. he is a good taxi driver

4. albert works for a large taxi company

5. the name of the taxi company is Lightning Taxi Service

6. albert drives a taxi six days a week

7. he meets fascinating people from many different places

8. albert really loves his work

WRITER'S NOTE: Using Capital Letters

On the Web
Try Unit 1
Activity 5

Proper Nouns

In English, the name of a specific person, place, or thing always begins with a capital letter. These types of words are called proper nouns. *George Washington* is the name of a specific person. *San Francisco* is the name of a specific place. *Pepsi* is the name of a specific thing. Can you think of more examples?

Incorrect:	My friend john works in chicago.
Correct:	My friend John works in Chicago. *(a specific person, a specific place)*
Incorrect:	lucille and robby drink coca-cola.
Correct:	Lucille and Robby drink Coca-Cola. *(specific people, a specific thing)*

Common Nouns

Common nouns do not begin with a capital letter. They begin with a small letter. Some examples of common nouns are *car, computer, garage, snow, television.*

More Capital Letters

In English, many other kinds of words begin with capital letters. Here are some examples.

Days of the week

Incorrect:	My birthday is on monday.
Correct:	My birthday is on Monday.

Months

Incorrect:	The shortest month of the year is february.
Correct:	The shortest month of the year is February.

Languages

Incorrect:	Sireesha speaks hindi.
Correct:	Sireesha speaks Hindi.

Countries

Incorrect:	My father is from thailand.
Correct:	My father is from Thailand.

(NOTE: See Appendix 3 for capitalization rules.)

WRITER'S NOTE: Question Marks

WWW

**On the Web
Try Unit 1
Activity 1**

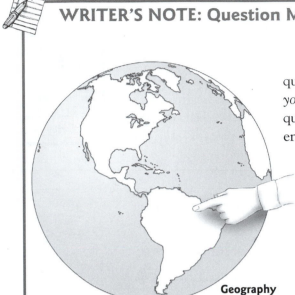

Geography

In English, some sentences end with a question mark (?). *Do you understand this? Do you have any questions?* These are examples of questions. They have a question mark at the end.

Incorrect:	Is Brazil a large country.
Correct:	Is Brazil a large country?
Incorrect:	Where do you live.
Correct:	Where do you live?

Activity 6 | **Geography Quiz**

How well do you know geography? Use the words below to write questions about geography. Then write the answers in complete sentences. Make sure the words are in the correct order. Be careful to use capital letters and punctuation. The first one has been done for you.

1. what / the capital / of brazil / is

   Question: ___What is the capital of Brazil?_____

   Answer: ___The capital of Brazil is Brasilia._____

2. is / what city / the white house in

   Question: _____

   Answer: _____

3. what country / the nile river in / is

   Question: _____

   Answer: _____

4. what city / is / the eiffel tower in

Question: _____

Answer: _____

5. what / the biggest city / in mexico / is

Question: _____

Answer: _____

6. where / are / the andes mountains

Question: _____

Answer: _____

7. is / what / the capital of saudi arabia

Question: _____

Answer: _____

8. what / the biggest province / is / in canada

Question: _____

Answer: _____

WRITER'S NOTE: Prepositions of Place—*AT, ON,* and *IN*

Three important prepositions are *AT, ON,* and *IN.* These prepositions have many meanings, but one important function is to indicate location.

AT is used with specific locations such as

- business names   (I work at First Union Bank.)
- street names with a house   (I live at 915 W. Norcross Street.)
  or business number

ON is used with

- street names (without the house   (I live on W. Norcross Street.)
  or business number).

IN is used with

- town or city names   (I live in Houston.)

- state names   (I live in Texas.)

- larger region names   (I live in the South.)

- country names   (I live in the U.S.)

AT = an exact or specific location   **She works at First United Bank.**

ON = a street (without a house number)   **The bank is on Greet Street.**

IN = a city, state, country, larger area   **The bank is in San Diego.**

Why the pyramid for *at*, *in*, and *on*? The pyramid design here is especially good to show the difference in meaning for *at*, *on*, and *in* for place. The top of the pyramid is a point. It is a very small, specific place. We use *at* for a specific place. We use *on* for the next largest place. Finally, we use *in* in English for the largest places. Look at the examples to the right of the triangle. We use *at* for the bank, which is a specific place. We use *on* for the street, which is a larger place. We use *in* for the city, which is an even larger place.

| Activity 7 | **Choosing the Correct Preposition** |

Read this paragraph about banks in a small town. Underline the correct prepositions.

Paragraph 1

Banks in a Small Town

EXAMPLE PARAGRAPH

It is surprising that Nelson has seven banks. Nelson is a small town (**1.** at, in, on) California. There are only about 36,000 people (**2.** at, in, on) this town. However, there are three banks, and each bank has at least two branches. The banks are National, First California, and Trust. National Bank has branches (**3.** at, in, on) 60 Green Street and (**4.** at, in, on) Hanks Avenue. First California Bank has branches (**5.** at, in, on) Princeton Street and (**6.** at, in, on) Lee Road. Trust Bank has branches (**7.** at, in, on) 27 Temple Street, (**8.** at, in, on) Whispering Street, and (**9.** at, in, on) 445 Orange Avenue. No one understands why there are seven banks (**10.** at, in, on) a small town like Nelson, California.

WRITER'S NOTE: Exclamation Points

You use an exclamation point (!) to show emphasis or emotion about something. Exclamation points are not used often, but when a sentence expresses surprise, it is appropriate to use an exclamation point.

Simple Fact:	It's snowing.
With Surprise:	It's snowing!
Incorrect:	I won the lottery last night?
Correct:	I won the lottery last night!

Activity 8   **Statement, Question, or Exclamation**

Read each sentence. If it is a statement, put S on the line and a period (.) at the end of the sentence. If it is a question, write Q on the line and put a question mark (?) at the end of the question. If it is an exclamation, write E on the line and put an exclamation point (!) at the end of the sentence. The first two have been done for you.

1. ___Q___ How many days are in a month?

2. ___S___ The answer depends on the month.

3. _____ Some months have thirty days

4. _____ An example of this is September

5. _____ Other months have thirty-one days

6. _____ Examples of this are July and December

7. _____ What month never has thirty days

8. _____ The answer is February

9. _____ February usually has twenty-eight days

10. _____ Everyone in my family was born in February

February						
SUN	MON	TUE	WED	THU	FRI	SAT
						1
2	3	4	5	6	7	8
9	10	11	12	13	14	15
16	17	18	19	20	21	22
23	24	25	26	27	28	

Activity 9   **Interview: Writing Information**

Copy the questions on the lines. Be sure to use capital letters and question marks. Ask a classmate the questions. Then write your classmate's answers. Use capital letters and periods.

1. what is your name

   Question: _____

   Answer: _____

2. where are you from

   Question: _____

   Answer: _____

3. where do you live

   Question: _____

   Answer: _____

4. how many people are in your family

   Question: _____

   Answer: _____

5. do you have a car

   Question: _____

   Answer: _____

6. what food do you like to eat

   Question: _____

   Answer: _____

7. what is your favorite place to visit

Question: _____

Answer: _____

8. what is your favorite movie

Question: _____

Answer: _____

Editing

Activity 10   **Editing Scrambled Sentences**

Here are some sentences and questions about Costa Rica. The words and phrases in each sentence are scrambled. First, put the sentence or question parts in the correct order. Then add capital letters. Finally, add a period, a question mark, or an exclamation point.

Topic: Write about a country.

1. costa rica / where / is

   _____

2. in central america / a country / costa rica / is

   _____

3. between panama / and nicaragua / it / is

   _____

4. it / is / between the pacific ocean / and the atlantic ocean

   _____

5. approximately two million / is / the population

   _____

6. many tourists / there / go

_____

7. wild animals / they / see / in the jungle

_____

8. in the world / the most beautiful country / it is

_____

9. want to visit / I / this beautiful country

_____

10. costa rica / do you want / to visit

_____

| Activity 11 | Guided Writing Practice |

Answer the following questions and write eight to ten sentences about a country. Use capital letters, periods, question marks, and exclamation points correctly.

Topic: Write about a country.

1. What country do you want to visit? _____

2. Why do you want to visit this country? _____

_____

_____

3. Where is this country located? _____

_____

4. How big is this country? _____

_____

5. What is the capital of this country? _____

_____

6. What is one famous monument or important location in this country? _____

_____

7. Briefly describe this monument or location. _____ _____

_____

_____

8. What do you know about the food in this country? _____

_____

_____

THE PARTS OF A SENTENCE

Every English sentence must have a subject and a verb.

The Simple Sentence

The basic sentence pattern that you are studying in this unit is called a **simple sentence**. A simple sentence has one subject (S) and verb (V) combination. Usually there is a noun or pronoun object (O) or other information after the verb.

simple sentence: S + V + O

Subject	+	Verb	+	Object	+	Other Information
a. Maria Simms		plays		the piano		well.
b. She		practices		the piano		every day.
c. Maria		likes		classical piano music		a lot.
d. She		enjoys		listening		to German music.

SENTENCE DEVELOPMENT

---

simple sentence: S + V

Subject	+	Verb	+	Object	+	Other Information
e. Maria		plays				extremely well.
f. She		practices				for three hours.
g. Maria		goes				to piano class every day.

- Some verbs, such as *like* and *enjoy*, must have an object after them. [These are called transitive verbs. In a dictionary, these are marked with the letters *vt*.] (Incorrect: Maria likes a lot.)

- Some verbs, such as *go* and *arrive*, can never have an object after them. [These are called intransitive verbs. In a dictionary, these are marked with the letters *vi*.] (Incorrect: Maria goes piano class.)

- Some verbs, such as *play* and *practice*, can have an object or not have an object. [In a dictionary, these are marked with only the letter *v*.]

GRAMMAR AND SENTENCE STRUCTURE:
Subjects, Verbs, and Objects

On the Web
Try Unit 1
Activity 2
Activity 7

In English, every sentence has two main parts: the subject and the verb. As you study the following simple sentences, look for this pattern.

Subject

The subject is the person or thing that does the action. The subject comes before the verb. Look at these simple sentences. The subjects are underlined.

<u>Maria Simms</u> plays the piano.

<u>She</u> practices the piano every day.

Maria likes classical piano music a lot.

Maria goes to piano class every week. (no object)

Verb

The verb is usually the action word in the sentence. The verb comes after the subject. Examples of verbs are *go, speak, write, swim,* and *watch.* Some verbs do not have much action. Examples are *be (am, is, are, was, were), like, want,* and *need.* Look at these simple sentences. The verbs are circled.

Maria Simms (plays) the piano.

She (practices) the piano every day.

Maria (likes) classical piano music a lot.

Maria (goes) to piano class every week. (no object)

Object

The object is the thing or person after the verb. The object answers the question *who?* or *what?* The object is the thing or person that receives the action of the verb. Look at these simple sentences. The objects are in boxes. (These objects are also called direct objects.)

Maria Simms plays the piano.

She practices the piano every day.

Maria likes classical piano music a lot.

Maria goes to piano class every week. (no object)

Fragments: Checking for the Subject and the Verb

Every sentence should have a subject and a verb. It is easy for student writers to leave out the subject or the verb. A sentence without a subject or without a verb is called a fragment. A fragment is a piece of a sentence.

Incorrect: John is my brother. Works at Ames Bank in Miami. (*no subject*)

Correct: John (is) my brother. He (works) at Ames Bank in Miami.

Incorrect: Most Japanese people a white car. (*no verb*)

Correct: Most Japanese people (have) a white car.

Correct: Most Japanese people (drive) a white car.

When you write, check to make sure each sentence has a subject for the verb and a verb for the subject.

Commands

In command (imperative) sentences, the subject is *you.* However, the word *you* is not usually stated.

Examples: Open the door now! (NOT: *You* open the door now!)

Don't say that word! (NOT: *You* don't say that word!)

Activity 12   Subjects and Verbs

Read these sentences about making tuna salad. Underline each subject and circle each verb.

1. Tuna salad is easy to make.

2. The ingredients are simple and cheap.

3. Two ingredients are tuna fish and mayonnaise.

4. I also use onions, salt, and pepper.

5. First, I cut up the onions.

6. Then I add the tuna fish and the mayonnaise.

7. Finally, I add some salt and a lot of pepper.

8. Tuna salad is my favorite food!

Activity 13   Sentence or Fragment

Read each group of words. If it is a fragment, write F on the line. If it is a complete sentence, write S on the line. If it is a question, write Q. The first two have been done for you.

On the Web
Try Unit 1
Activity 3

1. ___S___ Billy Mitchell lives in a big apartment.

2. ___F___ My mother breakfast every morning.

3. _____ Is incredibly delicious.

4. _____ Does Carol have a car?

5. _____ They my cousins from Miami.

6. _____ You a student.

7. _____ Michael likes classical music.

8. _____ Nancy and Jeanine very best friends.

9. _____ The girls play soccer after school.

10. _____ I am from Colombia.

GRAMMAR AND SENTENCE STRUCTURE: The Verb *Be*

The most frequently used verb in the English language is the verb *be*. The verb has five main forms: *am, is, are, was,* and *were*.

I <u>am</u> a student.

My writing <u>is</u> good.

My friends <u>are</u> here.

I <u>was</u> a good student in kindergarten.

The questions on the quiz <u>were</u> difficult.

There are four commonly used sentence patterns for the verb *be*. The information that follows the verb be is usually an adjective (a word that describes a noun), a noun, or a place phrase.

1. **Subject** + *be* + **adjective**

   This tuna salad   is   delicious.

2. **Subject** + *be* + **noun (often a profession)**

   This tuna salad   is   a delicious dish.

3. **Subject** + *be* + **place phrase**

   The tuna salad   is   on the table.

When you begin a sentence with *There*, the subject is after *be*.

4. **There** + *be* + **subject** + **(extra information: usually place or time)**

   There   is   a tuna salad sandwich   on the table.

   There   were   two empty plates   on the table this morning.

   There   was   a big sale on canned tuna   last week.

Note: More practice on writing sentences with *There is / There are* can be found on p. 74 in Unit 3.

When you have a sentence with *be + verb + ing*, then *be* is not the main verb.

Example: I am studying English.   ➔   verb: *am studying* (from *study*)

but

I am a student.   ➔   verb: *am* (from *be*)

Activity 14   Subjects and Verbs

Read these eight sentences. Underline the subject and circle the verb.

EXAMPLE PARAGRAPH

(**1.**) There are four books on the table. (**2.**) The two large books are textbooks.

(**3.**) The grammar book is green. (**4.**) The composition book is next to the grammar book. (**5.**)It is blue. (**6.**) The other two books are smaller. (**7.**) They are workbooks.

(**8.**)The textbooks are easy, but the workbooks are difficult.

Activity 15   Identifying Words and Phrases

Look at the sentences in Activity 14. Identify the words or phrases in circles as an adjective, *a* noun, *or a* place phrase.

1. on the table = _____

2. textbooks = _____

3. green = _____

4. next to the grammar book =_____

5. blue =_____

6. smaller =_____

7. workbooks =_____

8. easy =_____

9. difficult =_____

Activity 16   **Sentence Completion**

Read these sets of three sentences. Complete the sentences with the correct form of be.

1. There _____ seven colors in a rainbow. These colors _____ red, orange,

   yellow, green, blue, indigo, and violet. My favorite rainbow color _____ green.

2. There _____ twenty-six letters in the English alphabet. Twenty-one of these letters

   _____ consonants. The other five letters _____ vowels.

3. There _____ different students in my class. Five students _____ from

   Venezuela. Only one student _____ from China.

4. There _____ an insect on the window. It _____ a caterpillar.

   It _____ light yellow, and it has spots on it.

5. There _____ a huge map of the world on the wall in our classroom. The water areas

   _____ light blue. The land areas _____ various colors.

WRITER'S NOTE: Using Supporting Ideas with *There is/There are* Sentences

Sometimes a simple paragraph begins with a *There is/There are* sentence. This sentence tells the reader that something exists. A good paragraph also contains sentences that are related to the topic or idea in the first sentence.

EXAMPLE PARAGRAPH

There is a huge map of the world on the wall in our classroom. The water areas are light blue. All of the oceans, seas, and lakes are light blue. The land areas are various colors. The countries are red, yellow, green, blue, and tan. Heavy black dots are the capital cities. This map is so big that students in the back of the room can see all of the country names.

1. The first sentence begins with *There is. . . .* It tells the reader about a map.

2. The second sentence describes a part of the map. (water areas)

3. The third sentence describes a part of the map. (examples of water areas)

4. The fourth sentence describes a part of the map. (land areas)

5. The fifth sentence describes a part of the map. (examples of land areas)

6. The sixth sentence describes a part of the map. (capital cities)

7. The last sentence talks about how big the map is and how all the students can see it.

Activity 17   Writing Paragraph Beginnings

In numbers 1–3, write two additional sentences that are related to the first sentence. In numbers 4–6, write a sentence with there is/there are *and then add two related sentences. Follow the examples from Activity 16.*

1. There are _____ * people in my family. _____

_____

_____

_____

2. There are _____ * students in my English class. _____

_____

_____

_____

3. There are many unique animals in a zoo. _____

_____

_____

_____

4. _____

_____

_____

_____

5. _____

_____

_____

_____

6. _____

_____

_____

_____

*Add the correct number.

| **Activity 18** | **Identifying Words and Phrases** |

Read the simple sentences in this paragraph. Identify the underlined words as a subject (S), verb (V), or adjective (ADJ). The first one has been done for you.

Paragraph 2

EXAMPLE PARAGRAPH

Making Tuna Salad

          S
<u>Tuna salad</u> is easy to make. The ingredients are <u>simple</u> and <u>cheap</u>. <u>Two ingredients</u> are

tuna fish and mayonnaise. <u>I</u> also use onions, salt, and pepper. First, I <u>cut up</u> the onions.

Then I <u>add</u> the tuna fish and the mayonnaise. Finally, I add some salt and a lot of pepper.

Tuna salad <u>is</u> my <u>favorite</u> food!

SENTENCES IN PARAGRAPHS

You can put sentences together to make a paragraph. All the sentences in a paragraph are about the same topic.

WRITER'S NOTE: Sentences and Paragraphs

A group of words that tell about one idea is called a sentence. A group of sentences that tell about one topic or one idea is called a paragraph.

Look at the sentences in Activity 12 and Activity 18 again. How are they different? In Activity 12, eight sentences are in a list. In Activity 18, the same eight sentences are not in a list. They are in a special format. This format is called a paragraph. What do you know about paragraphs? You will study much more about paragraphs beginning in Unit 2.

| Activity 19 | **Subject–Verb Word Order** |

Underline the correct subject and verb combination in parentheses ( ). Remember that the subject comes before the verb.

On the Web
Try Unit 1
Activity 4

Paragraph 3

SEXAMPLE PARAGRAPH

A Great Place to Work

(**1.** Caroline Jimenez works / Works Caroline Jimenez) at Anderson Supermarket. (**2.** Works she / She works) there on Mondays and Thursdays. She does not work there on Wednesdays because (**3.** attends she / she attends) classes at Jefferson Community College. On her work days, (**4.** Caroline wakes up / Wakes up Caroline) at 6 A.M. (**5.** She starts / Starts she) work at 8 A.M. (**6.** Works she / She works) from 8 A.M. to 5 P.M. (**7.** Is her lunch break / Her lunch break is) from 12:30 to 1:30. (**8.** Caroline likes / Likes Caroline) her job. (**9.** Enjoys she / She enjoys) meeting people. (**10.** She loves / Loves she) her co-workers. For Caroline, (**11.** is Anderson Supermarket / Anderson Supermarket is) a great place to work.

WRITER'S NOTE: The Title of a Paragraph

What is the title of this textbook? Look on the front cover. Write the title here.

_____

What is the title of Paragraph 1? Write the title here.

_____

A title gives you information about what is in a book, a song, a movie, or a paragraph. Here are some rules to follow when you write a title for your paragraphs.

1. A good title is usually very short. Sometimes it is only one word. *Frankenstein*, *Cinderella*, and *Titanic* are all titles. Can you think of other one-word titles?

2. A good title is usually not a complete sentence. *Jobs for the Future, A World Traveler*, and *An Old Family Photo* are all titles of paragraphs in this book. These titles are not complete sentences. Can you think of some titles of books you have read?

3. A good title catches the reader's interest. It tells the reader about the main topic, but it doesn't tell about everything in the paragraph. *A Long Flight, An Important Invention*, and *Smoking in Public Places* are all titles of paragraphs in this book. Each one gives you a good idea of what the paragraph will be about. However, it doesn't give you all the information. You must read the paragraph to find out more.

4. A good title also follows special capitalization rules. Never capitalize the entire title. Instead, the first letter of the first word is always capitalized. Only capitalize the first letter of the important words in the title. Do not capitalize a preposition or an article unless it is the first word.

5. A good title does not have a period at the end.

Activity 20   Working with Titles

Each of these titles breaks one of the rules listed. Rewrite each one correctly. Be prepared to share your answers with your classmates and explain which rule(s) the incorrect title breaks.

1. Today Was the Best day of My Life

   _____

2. THE COMBUSTION ENGINE

   _____

3. A Handbook For International Students In Canada

   _____

4. Digging for Gold in California.

   _____

5. My Paragraph

   _____

6. How to Make a Phone Call to Another Country Without Spending a Lot of Money

   _____

Activity 21   **Editing Simple Sentences**

Read these ten sentences about world geography. Some of the sentences are fragments (missing subject or missing verb) or have errors with punctuation or capitalization. If the sentence is correct, write C on the line. If the sentence contains an error, write X on the line and tell what the error is. Then write the correct sentence below. Follow the examples.

On the Web
Try Unit 1
Activity 6

Examples:

X (fragment—verb missing) _____ Mexico not near Great Britain.

Mexico is not near Great Britain. _____

X (capitalization) _____ The Statue of Liberty is in new york.

The Statue of Liberty is in New York. _____

1. _____ Burundi is in africa.

_____

_____

2. _____ Canada bigger than the United States.

_____

_____

3. _____ A popular city in Florida is Miami?

_____

_____

4. _____ Nepal is north of India.

_____

_____

5. _____ Visits the Mayan ruins in Central America every year!

_____

_____

6. _____ Bolivia no seaports.

_____

_____

7. _____ Three main groups of people live in Malaysia.

_____

_____

8. _____ Austria and Hungary in Europe.

_____

_____

9. _____ Is between Mexico and Canada.

_____

_____

10. _____ Of Thailand is about 30,000,000.

_____

_____

Editing

| Activity 22 | **Editing: Grammar and Sentence Review** |

Read the following paragraph. There are nine mistakes: four (4) missing be *verbs, two (2) missing subjects, two (2) capitalization mistakes, and one (1) punctuation mistake. Find and correct the mistakes. The first one has been done for you.*

Paragraph 4

EXAMPLE PARAGRAPH

The Beauty of Tuscany

Tuscany ^is a beautiful region in Italy. Is famous for cities such as florence, Siena, and

Pisa. The appenine Hills in Tuscany? Tuscany also famous for wine making. For example,

Chianti and Montalcino wines very popular and tasty. Tuscany has so many interesting

places to see. Is a wonderful place to visit!

Word Build•ing (wûrd bĭl′dĭng) *n.*

Activity 23   Word Building

Study the following word forms. In the sentences on the right, choose the best word and write it in the blank space. Be sure to use the right form of the verb. The first one has been done for you. (Note: The word in bold is the original word that appears in the unit.)

Noun	Verb	Adjective	Sentence Practice
addi<u>tion</u>	**add**	Ø	1. She ___*adds*___ sugar to her coffee.
			2. We plan to build an _____ to our home.
attend<u>ance</u>	**attend**	Ø	3. The teacher checks the students' _____ every day.
			4. Do you want to _____ the concert tomorrow?
popular<u>ity</u>	Ø	**popular**	5. Britney is a _____ singer.
			6. The _____ of motorcycles is incredible!
happi<u>ness</u>	Ø	happy	7. She is very _____ because it is her birthday.
			8. The key to _____ is not easy.
work	**work**	Ø	9. My sisters _____ in a supermarket.
			10. Do you enjoy your _____?

Noun endings: -tion, -ance, -ity, -ness

Building Better Sentences

Correct and varied sentence structure is essential to the quality of your writing. For further practice, go to Practice 1 on page 236 in Appendix 16.

Activity 24   **Original Writing Practice**

Choose ONE of the practices below. For the practice you choose:

1. *Read the first question.*
2. *Fill in the answer. This will be the topic.*
3. *Then answer the questions about the topic. Be sure to use complete sentences with a subject and a verb.*
4. *After you write your sentences, check the spelling and grammar.*

Practice 1

Question 1a: What is your favorite food?

Answer 1a: My favorite food is _____ .

Question 1b: What country does this food come from?

Answer 1b: _____

_____

Question 1c: What ingredients are in this food?

Answer 1c: _____

_____

Question 1d: How do you prepare this food?

Answer 1d: _____

_____

Question 1e: Why do you like this food?

Answer 1e: _____

_____

Practice 2

Question 2a: What food do you like to cook?

Answer 2a: I like to cook _____ .

Question 2b: What ingredients do you need?

Answer 2b: _____

_____

Question 2c: What is the first thing you do?

Answer 2c: _____

_____

Question 2d: What do you do next?

Answer 2d: _____

_____

Question 2e: How long does it take to prepare this food?

Answer 2e: _____

_____

Practice 3

Question 3a: Who is the most interesting person in your family?

Answer 3a: The most interesting person in my family is _____ .

Question 3b: Why is this person interesting?

Answer 3b: _____

_____

Question 3c: How old is this person?

Answer 3c: _____

_____

Question 3d: What does this person look like?

Answer 3d: _____

_____

Question 3e: Why do you like this person?

Answer 3e: _____

_____

EDITING

Good writers need editors to help them make their writing correct. For your writing in this book, you and your classmates (peers) are your editors.

WRITER'S NOTE: Self-Editing

An editor is someone who makes sure writing is correct. A good editor checks the grammar and punctuation. A good editor also makes sure the writing is clear and easy to understand. There should be two editors when you write a paragraph for class: you and a classmate. First, you will read your own work for mistakes. Then a classmate (a peer) will read your work and help you find ways to make it better.

WRITER'S NOTE: Peer Editing for the Writer

A peer is someone who is equal to you. Your peers are the other students in your class.

It is important to hear what other people think about your writing. You need to know if they can understand your ideas. A good way to make sure that your writing is clear is to let someone else read your paper and make suggestions about it. This is called peer editing.

This is what usually happens in peer editing:

1. Another person reads your writing.

2. That person gives you suggestions and ideas for making your paper better.

3. You listen carefully to what your peer says.

4. You may want to make the changes your peer suggests. If the comments are negative, remember that the comments are about the writing, not about you!

WRITER'S NOTE: Peer Editing for the Reader

When you read your classmate's paper, be polite. Choose your words carefully. Don't say, "This is bad grammar" or "What is this?" It's better to say, "You forgot to put the word *at*" or "What does this sentence mean?"

Say things the way you would want someone to tell you!

Activity 25   Peer Editing

Choose someone with whom you work well. Exchange books and look at Activity 24. Read each other's sentences. Then use Peer Editing Sheet 1 on page 253 to help you talk about your partner's writing.

JOURNAL WRITING

Many good writers write in a journal for practice and for ideas.

WRITER'S NOTE: Journal Writing—Write, Write, Write!

How can you become a better writer? The activities in this book will help you. The most important thing, however, is to write as much and as often as you can.

The Benefit of Practice

Think about people who can play tennis well. These people were excited about tennis. Perhaps they read books about tennis. They probably went to see a professional tennis match. These activities alone can't make people become good tennis players. They have to practice. It doesn't matter if at first they hit the ball the wrong way. The most important thing is to hit the ball again and again. This is how people get better at tennis.

In some ways, you are like the tennis player. You want to be a good writer. Reading this book and doing the activities are helpful. Reading books and articles will help you, too. One of the best ways to become a good writer in English is to write as much as possible and as often as possible.

Practice in a Journal

An excellent way to practice is to write in a journal. A journal is a notebook in which you write things regularly. You practice expressing yourself in written English.

In a journal, you choose a specific topic and write about it. You try to express your ideas about the topic so that readers can understand what you mean. Journal topics can be general or specific. Here are some topics for journal writing:

> *General topics:*   sports, swimming, food, pets, travel, fashion, music
>
> *Specific topics:*   my favorite sport, why I am a vegetarian, my first airplane trip

Teacher Response

Your teacher will read your journal from time to time. Your teacher won't mark all of the grammar mistakes. A journal uses informal language. It's like a conversation between the writer and the teacher (reader). If you write about a city, don't take information from a book. Instead, write about why you want to visit that city or about the first time you visited it.

Your teacher may write some comments in your journal. Your teacher might make one or two comments about the language, especially if you repeat the same mistake.

If you have any questions, you can ask your teacher in the journal. For example, if you want to know if you used a grammar point or a vocabulary word correctly, you can write a question in your journal.

SAMPLE JOURNAL

March 21

Sometimes I feel lonely here. My parents are far away, but my brother is here. His name is Nelson. He is two years older than I am. He wants to study business administration. He looks like my father. He is 22 years old.

Before we came here, Nelson and I went to New York City. We visited some cousins there. Hotels in New York expensive. We stayed with our cousins. That saved us a lot of money.

I don't my cousins very often, so I was happy. Sometimes I feel bad because I don't know them very well.

This is interesting information. I didn't know that your brother is at this school, too. Do you live together? I've been to New York City, too, and I know that hotels are VERY expensive there.

Grammar: I circled two places where you forgot to put a verb. Can you think of some verbs for those sentences?

It was easy to understand the message of your writing here. Keep up the good work!

Activity 26   **Journal Writing**

EXTRA WRITING

Here are ten ideas for journal writing. Write about as many as you can. Follow your teacher's directions. (We recommend that you skip a line after each line that you write. This gives your teacher a place to write comments.)

1. Write about your favorite pet. Why do you like this animal? Do you have one at home? What does the animal look like? What is its name? How old is it?

2. Write about your favorite type of weather. Why do you like this weather? What kinds of activities do you do in this weather?

3. Write about your mother or your father. Include his/her name, age, and occupation. What kind of personality does your mother or father have?

4. Write about a toy you remember from your childhood. What kind of toy was it? How long did you have it? Who gave it to you? Do you still have it? If not, what happened to it?

5. Write about your experience learning English. Why are you studying English? How do you feel about English? What is easy for you to understand in English? What are some difficulties you have in English?

6. Write about your favorite type of fashion in clothing. What kind is it? Why do you like it?

7. Write about an "extreme" sport, such as bungee jumping. How do you feel about this sport? Do you want to try this sport? Why or why not? Describe the types of people who enjoy these kinds of sports.

8. What do you miss about your country? Write about some things that you cannot find in the United States.

9. Write about your home. How many rooms are in your home? What color is it? How old is it? Do you like it? What is your favorite room?

10. Write about what you do in your leisure (free) time. Who do you spend the time with? What activities do you do? How long do you spend doing these activities? Are your free-time activities the same during the week and on weekends?

▶ MORE WRITING

For extra writing practice, see the activities in Unit 8, Appendix 17, and the *Great Sentences* website: http://esl.college.hmco.com/students.

Connecting Sentences and Paragraphs

GOAL: To learn about paragraph structure

GRAMMAR AND SENTENCE STRUCTURE: Adjectives; subject pronouns; possessive adjectives

SENTENCES: USING ADJECTIVES

You already know that a sentence must have a subject and a verb. (Remember from Unit 1 that a sentence without a subject or without a verb is called a fragment.) However, you can make a sentence much more interesting if you add descriptive words. These descriptive words are called adjectives. They describe nouns.

GRAMMAR AND SENTENCE STRUCTURE:
Word Order: Adjectives Before Nouns

Nouns are the names of people, places, things, or ideas. Examples are *teacher*, *doctor*, *student*, *city*, *park*, *cat*, *book*, and *pencil*.

Adjectives are words that describe nouns. Examples are *good* teacher, *busy* doctor, *new* student, *crowded* city, *green* park, *fat* cat, *heavy* book, and *yellow* pencil.

A simple way to combine two short sentences when there is an adjective is to put the adjective before the noun. Look at the following examples.

Two Short Sentences	Better Writing

I have a <u>cat</u>. It is <u>fat</u>.
     NOUN   ADJ.
	I have a <u>fat</u> <u>cat</u>.
	          ADJ.NOUN

This is my <u>car</u>. It is <u>new</u>.
     NOUN   ADJ.
	This is my <u>new</u> <u>car</u>.
	          ADJ. NOUN

Mr. Vicks is a <u>teacher</u>. He is <u>excellent</u>.
          NOUN   ADJ.
	Mr. Vicks is an <u>excellent</u> <u>teacher</u>.
	                    ADJ. NOUN

Rachel draws <u>small</u> <u>pictures</u>. She draws <u>ink</u> <u>pictures</u>.
          ADJ.   NOUN   ADJ.   NOUN
	Rachel draws <u>small</u> <u>ink</u> <u>pictures</u>.
	          ADJ. ADJ. NOUN

Careful! Be sure to put the adjective before the noun, not after.

Incorrect: I have a car red with a top gray.

Correct: I have a red car with a gray top.

Incorrect: We ate salad green with potatoes fried.

Correct: We ate green salad with fried potatoes.

Careful! Adjectives do not have a plural form to describe plural nouns.

Incorrect: There are rares books in the library.

Correct: There are rare books in the library.

Incorrect: Do you like populars songs?

Correct: Do you like popular songs?

(See Appendix 15 for more about order of adjectives.)

Editing

Activity 1   ▮ **Editing: Nouns and Adjectives**

Combine the following sentences. You will have to eliminate a few words. Remember to use a capital letter at the beginning and a period at the end. The first one has been done for you.

**On the Web
Try Unit 2
Activity 1**

1. Robert owns a Ferrari. The Ferrari is red.

   Robert owns a red Ferrari.

2. I don't like this weather. The weather is humid.

   _____

3. Paris is a city in France. This city is beautiful.

_____

4. Ali has a job. The job is part-time.

_____

5. They like to drink cola. The cola is diet.

_____

6. Marian reads folk tales. They are international.

_____

7. My mother grows roses. The roses are big. The roses are beautiful.

_____

8. Gillian works for a company. The company is small. The company is independent.

_____

9. My grandparents live in a town. The town is small. It is a farming town.

_____

10. Sharon rents a house on Smith Street. The house is tiny. The house is gray.

_____

GRAMMAR AND SENTENCE STRUCTURE:
Word Order: Adjectives After the Verb *Be*

You have learned that adjectives come before the noun they describe.

The <u>young boy</u> carried the <u>heavy box</u>.
ADJ. NOUN   ADJ. NOUN

In this sentence, *young* describes boy and *heavy* describes box.

Complements

Adjectives can be used in another way. If the main verb of a sentence is a form of *be*, the adjective can come *after* the verb. The adjective is called a *complement*.

The <u>boy</u> is <u>young</u>.   The <u>box</u> is <u>heavy</u>.
   NOUN   ADJ.   NOUN   ADJ.

My <u>uncle</u> is <u>rich</u>.   <u>Paris</u> is <u>beautiful</u>.
   NOUN   ADJ.   NOUN   ADJ.

That <u>music</u> is <u>loud</u>!   <u>Jim</u> is <u>sleepy</u>.
   NOUN   ADJ.   NOUN   ADJ.

That <u>house</u> is <u>big</u>.   That <u>house</u> is <u>green</u>.   That <u>house</u> is <u>big</u> and <u>green</u>.
   NOUN   ADJ.   NOUN   ADJ.   NOUN   ADJ.   ADJ.

Adjectives are very important in writing, so be sure that you use them correctly.

Activity 2 — Practice with Adjectives

On the Web
Try Unit 2
Activity 2

Read the following paragraph. There are ten adjectives in the paragraph. Underline them. If you need help finding the adjectives, look at the numbers in parentheses on the left side of the paragraph. These numbers tell you how many adjectives are in each line. The first one has been done for you.

Paragraph 5

EXAMPLE PARAGRAPH

My Dream Vacation

(2)   I have a dream to visit Alaska. The weather is <u>beautiful</u> there. I love cold weather.

(1)   When the temperature is low, I have energy! I also want to visit Alaska because I

(3)   love nature. Alaska is **pure** and natural. I dream about its **scenic** landscape. In

(1)   addition, there are wild

       animals. Finally, I want

(1)   to learn important infor-

(1)   mation about the **native**

       people of Alaska. I hope

(1)   to visit this wonderful

       state soon.

pure: clean; not polluted
scenic: having a beautiful natural landscape
native: born in a certain place; originated

WHAT IS A PARAGRAPH?

In Unit 1, you studied sentences. A **sentence** is a group of words that expresses a complete thought. You learned that a sentence has two main parts: the subject and the verb. The words in a sentence are in a special order.

Most people write much more than one sentence. Sometimes they write a paragraph. A **paragraph** is a group of sentences. All of the sentences in a paragraph are about one specific topic.

A paragraph has three main parts: the topic sentence, the body, and a concluding sentence.

The **topic sentence** is one sentence that tells the main idea of the whole paragraph. This sentence is usually the first sentence of the paragraph.

The **body** of a paragraph has sentences with information that supports the topic sentence. It is important to remember that *every* sentence in the body must be connected in some way to the topic sentence.

In addition to the topic sentence and the body, paragraphs generally have a third part: a **concluding sentence**. The concluding sentence is the end of the paragraph. It is a brief summary of the information in the paragraph. Some paragraphs, especially short paragraphs, do not have a concluding sentence.

WORKING WITH THE WHOLE PARAGRAPH

Let's see how the parts of a paragraph work together to make a good paragraph that is easy to read.

WRITER'S NOTE: Topic Sentence

Every good paragraph has a topic sentence. If there is no topic sentence, the reader may be confused because the ideas will not be organized clearly. When you write a paragraph, remember to use a topic sentence. It gives the general topic of the whole paragraph.

Activity 3   **Paragraph Study**

Read the following two paragraphs. Answer the questions that follow.

Paragraph 6

**On the Web
Try Unit 2
Activity 3**

My Favorite Color

   It is obvious that my favorite color is blue. I have six blue shirts. I wear blue jeans almost every day. I have three pairs of light blue tennis shoes. I own a blue car, and my computer is blue. Other colors are nice, but I like blue the best.

1. How many sentences are in this paragraph? _____

2. What is the main topic of this paragraph? (Circle the letter of the answer.)

   a. The writer likes blue computers.

   b. The writer likes blue.

   c. The writer likes light blue clothes.

3. What is the topic sentence? Remember that the topic sentence tells the main idea of the whole paragraph. Write it here:

   _____

4. The writer gives five examples of blue things. What five blue things does the writer have? Write five sentences about these blue things. Follow the example.

   a. _The writer has six blue shirts._____

   b. _____

   c. _____

   d. _____

   e. _____

5. Sometimes paragraphs have a concluding sentence. A concluding sentence is a summary of the ideas in the paragraph. If there is a concluding sentence, write it here:

   _____

6. Read the paragraph again. Can you find at least two descriptive adjectives? Write them below.

   _____

Paragraph 7

The Franklin Building

I work in a popular building called the Franklin Building. This building is in **downtown** Atlanta. The Franklin Building is over 100 years old. It is made of dark red **brick**. It has many windows. The building has six **floors**. Each floor has a different company. Everyone likes the Franklin Building very much.

downtown: the center of a city (usually commercial/cultural)   **floors:** levels of a building
brick: small squares of baked clay used to build houses and buildings

1. How many sentences are in this paragraph?

    _____

2. What is the main topic of this paragraph? (Circle the letter of the answer.)

    a. information about a city

    b. information about a person

    c. information about a building

3. What is the topic sentence? Write it here:

    _____

    _____

    _____

    _____

4. Answer these questions in complete sentences.

    a. Where is the building?

    _____

    b. How old is the building?

    _____

    c. What color is the building?

    _____

    d. How many floors does the building have?

    _____

5. Sometimes paragraphs have a concluding sentence. A concluding sentence is a summary of the ideas in the paragraph. If there is a concluding sentence, write it here:

_____

_____

6. Read the paragraph again. Can you find at least four descriptive adjectives? Write them below.

_____

_____

WRITER'S NOTE: Indent the First Line of Every Paragraph

**On the Web
Try Unit 2
Activity 4**

    Look at the first line of Paragraph 6 on page 43. How is the formatting different from the other lines in the paragraph?

    Look at the first line of Paragraph 7 on page 44. Do you see how the first line is also moved in? This space is called an indentation. The action of making this space at the beginning of a paragraph is to **indent**.

    It is important to indent the first line of every paragraph. Always remember to indent!

Activity 4   **Copying a Paragraph**

On the lines below, copy the six sentences about spaghetti from Activity 3, Unit 1, pages 4–5. Be sure to indent the first line. Use correct punctuation at the end of each sentence. Give this paragraph a title. When you finish, read your new paragraph. Underline the topic sentence.

Paragraph 8

_____

_____

_____

_____

_____

_____

_____

_____

_____

_____

_____

_____

_____

_____

On the lines below, copy the eight sentences about the taxi driver from Activity 5, Unit 1, page 6. Be sure to indent the first line. Use correct punctuation at the end of each sentence. Give this paragraph a title. When you finish, read your new paragraph. Underline the topic sentence.

Paragraph 9

_____

_____

_____

_____

_____

_____

_____

_____

_____

_____

_____

| Activity 5 | **Writing an Original Paragraph** |

Answer the questions. Be sure to use complete sentences. When you finish, write your sentences in paragraph form on the lines provided below.

1. Who is your favorite singer? ___My favorite singer is_____

2. What country does he/she come from? _____

_____

3. What kind of music does he/she sing? _____

_____

4. What is your favorite song by this singer? _____

5. Why do you like this singer? _____

_____

Now write your sentences in paragraph form. Be sure to give your paragraph a title.

_____

_____

_____

_____

_____

_____

_____

_____

_____

_____

WORKING WITH TOPIC SENTENCES

Every paragraph must have a good topic sentence. The topic sentence gives the main idea of the paragraph. The topic sentence should not be too specific or too general. The topic sentence tells the reader what the paragraph is about.

Activity 6	**Topic Sentences**

Read each paragraph and the three topic sentences below it. Then choose the best topic sentence and write it on the line. Read the paragraph again. Make sure that the topic sentence gives the main idea for the whole paragraph. Remember to indent!

Paragraph 10

Maria and Her Great Job

_____

_____ . She works at Papa Joe's Restaurant. She serves about sixty people

every day. Maria can remember all the dinner orders. If there is a problem with any of the food,

she takes it back to the kitchen immediately. Maria wants every customer to have a good meal

at the restaurant.

    a. My cousin Maria is an excellent server.

    b. My cousin Maria works at Papa Joe's Restaurant.

    c. Maria's customers do not eat big meals.

Paragraph 11

My Favorite City

_____

_____ . I love to see all the interesting things there. The city is big, exciting,

and full of life. I always visit the Empire State Building and the Statue of Liberty. I also visit

Chinatown. At night, I go to **shows** on Broadway. The food in the city is excellent, too. I truly

enjoy New York City.

show: live performance on stage

    a. I like to see the Empire State Building and the Statue of Liberty.

    b. New York is a very big city.

    c. My favorite city in the world is New York City.

Paragraph 12

Beautiful Snow?

_____

_____ . Snow is beautiful when it falls. After a few days, the snow isn't beautiful

anymore. It starts to melt, and the clean streets become **messy**. It is difficult to walk anywhere.

The **sidewalks** are slippery. Snow also causes traffic problems. Some roads are closed. Other

roads are **hard** to drive on safely. Drivers have more **accidents** on snowy roads. I understand

why some people like snow, but I don't like it very much.

messy: sloppy; dirty	**hard:** difficult
sidewalks: paved walkways on the side of roads	**accidents:** car crashes

    a. In December, it usually snows.

    b. Some people like snow, but I don't.

    c. I love snow.

Activity 7	**More Work with Topic Sentences**

*Read each paragraph and the four topic sentences below it. Then choose the best topic sentence
and write it on the line. Read the paragraph again. Make sure that the topic sentence gives the
main idea for the whole paragraph. Be sure to indent!*

Paragraph 13

Pasta, Pasta, Pasta

_____

_____ . Pasta tastes great. Sometimes I eat it **plain**. I also like it with butter

or **parmesan** cheese. Another reason I like pasta is the **variety**. Pasta includes spaghetti,

macaroni, vermicelli, ravioli, lasagna, and many other kinds. In addition, pasta is very easy

to prepare. I can make pasta in less than 10 minutes. Finally, pasta is a very healthy food for

me. A plate of pasta has about 300 **calories**, but it has only 3 grams of fat. I love to eat

pasta every day!

plain: with nothing added; simple	**variety:** many different kinds
parmesan: a hard, dry Italian cheese	**calories:** measurement of heat energy of food

a. Everybody loves pasta.

b. Spaghetti and macaroni are kinds of pasta.

c. Pasta is my favorite food.

d. Pasta comes from Italy.

Paragraph 14

Good Teachers

_____

_____ . First of all, good teachers are **patient**. They never rush their students. Good teachers explain things without getting **bored**. In addition, they are organized. They plan what happens in every class. Good teachers are also **encouraging**. They help students understand the subject. Finally, good teachers are fair. They treat all students the same. These are some of the most important qualities of good teachers.

patient: calm; untiring   **bored:** not interested   **encouraging:** helpful; comforting

a. All good teachers are patient.

b. Good teachers have special qualities.

c. I like my teachers.

d. Some teachers are good, but some teachers are not so good.

Paragraph 15

A Radio Station for Everyone

_____

_____ . Radio Station 97.5 FM plays Spanish music. For people who like rock music, there is Station 98.1. The music on Radio Station 101.5 is all jazz. Station 103.6 plays blues music during the day and jazz at night. Station 103.9 plays many different kinds of music. Young people listen to Station 105.7 for dance music. This city is lucky to have so many kinds of music stations.

a. This city offers radio stations for everyone.

b. This city does not have many Spanish music stations.

c. I do not like rock music very much.

d. I like jazz a lot.

GRAMMAR AND SENTENCE STRUCTURE:
Subject Pronouns

A pronoun is a word that takes the place of a noun. A subject pronoun comes before the verb, just like any subject usually does. In English, there are seven subject pronouns.

Singular	**Plural**
I	we
you	you
he / she / it	they

Examples with sentences:

Singular	**Plural**
I live in Panama.	We live in Panama.
You are from Africa.	You are from Africa.
He works in a factory.	They work in a factory.

Activity 8   **Subject Pronouns**

Read the following paragraph. Replace the nouns in parentheses with a subject pronoun. The first one has been done for you.

Paragraph 16

Two Doctors

Rosemarie Bertrand and Michael Scott are interesting people. Rosemarie is a doctor in

Scotland. (**1.** Rosemarie Bertrand) _____She_____ is married to Michael.

(**2.** Michael Scott) _____ is also a doctor. (**3.** Rosemarie and Michael)

_____ live in Edinburgh. (**4.** Edinburgh) _____ is a historic city.

Dr. Bertrand and Dr. Scott have an office together downtown. (**5.** The office) _____

is busy every day. (**6.** Rosemarie and Michael) _____ work hard five days a week.

On weekends, however, (**7.** Rosemarie and Michael) _____ like to travel to the

countryside. (**8.** The countryside) _____ is a beautiful and relaxing escape from

all their hard work.

On the Web
Try Unit 2
Activity 5

WRITER'S NOTE:
Writing About People: Proper Nouns and Subject Pronouns

When you write about a person, you use that person's name. The name is called a proper noun. (For more information about proper nouns, see p. 7.) Study these examples:

<u>George Woods</u> teaches at Briar Elementary School. <u>He</u> teaches math and science there.
　NOUN　　　　　　　　　　　　　　　　　　　　　　　　　PRONOUN

<u>Alisa</u> lives in the city. <u>She</u> likes the noise and the crowds.
　NOUN　　　　　　　　　　PRONOUN

It is correct to use a person's name when you write one or two sentences, but in a paragraph or in conversation, good writers and speakers do not use the person's name many times. Instead, they can use a subject **pronoun** (*I, you, he, she, it, we,* and *they*).

Remember: Do not repeat the proper noun many times. Replace it with a pronoun.

WORKING WITH THE BODY OF THE PARAGRAPH

Earlier in this unit you practiced topic sentences. Every topic sentence must have supporting sentences—these make up the body of the paragraph. This body of supporting sentences is directly related to the topic sentence. Supporting sentences give information about the topic sentence. Therefore, the supporting sentences are just as important as the topic sentence.

One mistake that many writers make is writing sentences that are not related to the topic sentence. Plan what your supporting information will be so that it is related to the topic sentence.

WRITER'S NOTE:
Supporting Sentences: The Body of a Paragraph

You have learned that a paragraph has three main parts: the topic sentence, the body, and the concluding sentence. Remember the body consists of sentences that give supporting information and ideas about the topic sentence. Therefore, it is important for *every* sentence to be related to the topic sentence.

Make sure that each sentence provides support, details, or examples for the ideas in the topic sentence. Cut out any unrelated or unconnected ideas!

| Activity 9 | **The Body of the Paragraph** |

Read each paragraph carefully. Underline the topic sentence. In each paragraph, one supporting sentence does not belong because it is not directly connected to the topic sentence. It does not fit the ideas in the paragraph. Put parentheses ( ) around the sentence that does not belong.

Paragraph 17

EXAMPLE PARAGRAPH

Keeping Score in American Football

Keeping **score** in American football is more difficult than keeping score in soccer. In soccer, each goal is **worth** one point. For example, if a team scores five goals in a game, then the team's score is five points. In American football, the scoring system is different. When a player carries the ball across the end zone, he scores a touchdown. A touchdown is worth six points. When a player kicks the football between the goal posts, that team gets one point or three points. Another sport that has easy scoring is basketball.

score: total; count
worth: equal to; valued at

Paragraph 18

EXAMPLE PARAGRAPH

Celsius and Fahrenheit Temperatures

Changing temperatures from Celsius to Fahrenheit is not difficult. First, **multiply** the Celsius temperature by 9. Then **divide** this answer by 5. When you finish, add 32 **degrees** to your answer. The result is the temperature in Fahrenheit. Many countries report temperatures in Celsius, but the United States uses Fahrenheit. For example, if the Celsius temperature is 20, you multiply 20 by 9. Then you divide the answer, 180, by 5. The result is 36. Next, add 32, and you have the correct Fahrenheit temperature. Now you know how to change a temperature from Celsius to Fahrenheit.

multiply: $2 \times 2 = 4$
divide: $15 \div 3 = 5$
degrees: units of measurement for temperature: $98° = 98$ degrees

Paragraph 19

Making **Chili**

Chili is an easy dish to prepare. Fried chicken is also easy to prepare. To make chili, cut up two large onions. Then fry them in a little vegetable oil. You can add fresh garlic and some **diced** chili peppers. When the onions are soft, add two pounds of **ground** beef. **Stir** the onions and beef until they are **fully** cooked. Sprinkle one tablespoon of red chili powder on top. Next, add four cups of diced tomatoes, two cups of water, and add one can of red beans. Finally, add salt and pepper. Cover the saucepan and cook over low heat for about one hour. If you follow this simple **recipe**, you will have a delicious **meal**!

chili: a thick stew made with meat, beans, and tomatoes
diced: cut into little squares
ground: broken into small pieces
stir: mix
fully: completely; entirely
recipe: directions for cooking food
meal: breakfast, lunch, or dinner

GRAMMAR AND SENTENCE STRUCTURE:
Possessive Adjectives

When you want to talk about something that belongs to someone or something, you use a possessive adjective. A possessive adjective shows possession. It answers questions such as *Whose house? Whose books? Whose television?*

In English, there are seven **possessive adjectives**: *my, your, his, her, its, our, their.* A possessive adjective always comes before a noun.

my	I live in <u>my</u> father's house.
your	Do you have <u>your</u> books?
his	He lives with <u>his</u> father.
her	She does not carry money in <u>her</u> purse.
its	Poor cat! It has a cut on <u>its</u> face.
our	We write all <u>our</u> papers on a computer.
their	They can bring <u>their</u> CDs.

Activity 10   **Possessive Adjectives**

Read the following paragraph. Write the missing possessive adjectives. The first one has been done for you.

Paragraph 20

Caroline and Her Sisters

Caroline has two sisters and one brother. (**1.**) _Their_____ names are Ashley, Margaret,

and Nick. Ashley and Margaret live with (**2.**) _____ parents. They are high school

students. Ashley likes to play sports. (**3.**) _____ favorite sport is softball. She is a

very good player. Margaret does not like sports, but she loves music. She plays (**4.**)

_____ guitar every afternoon after school. Ashley and Margaret have the same

friends. (**5.**) _____ friends go to the same school. (**6.**) _____ brother

Nick is in college. (**7.**) _____ major is business administration. Caroline's brother

and sisters are all very different, but she loves (**8.**) _____ siblings very much.

siblings: brothers and sisters

Activity 11 — Subject Pronouns and Possessive Adjectives

This paragraph contains many subject pronouns and possessive adjectives. Underline the correct forms in parentheses ( ). The first one has been done for you.

Paragraph 21

(I, <u>My</u>) Grandmother

On the Web
Try Unit 2
Activity 6

A very important person in (**1.** I, my) life is (**2.** I, my) grandmother. (**3.** She, Her) name is Evelyn Anna Kratz. (**4.** She, Her) life is very interesting. (**5.** She, Her) is 89 years old. (**6.** She, Her) comes from Poland. (**7.** She, Her) can speak English well, but (**8.** she, her) first language is Polish. My grandmother comes from a large family. (**9.** She, Her) has two brothers. (**10.** They, Their) names are Peter and John. (**11.** I, My) grandmother has two sisters, too. (**12.** They, Their) names are Karina and Maria. (**13.** I, My) like to listen to (**14.** my, her) grandmother's stories because (**15.** they, their) are so interesting. In (**16.** I, my) opinion, they are the most interesting stories in the world.

Activity 12 — More Practice with the Body of the Paragraph

Read the topic sentence and body of each paragraph carefully. In each paragraph, there are two sentences that do not belong. Find and underline these sentences.

Paragraph 22

The *New* States

Four U.S. states begin with the word *New*. New Hampshire, New Jersey, and New York are in the Northeast, but New Mexico is in the Southwest. Arizona is also in the Southwest. New Hampshire is a small state with about one million people. New Jersey is also a small state, but its population is about eight million people. The most **well-known** of the *New* states is New York. The population of New York is about twenty million. New Mexico is the largest of these four states, but its population is small. There are no states that begin with the word *Old*. Although all these states begin with *New*, they are all very different.

well-known: popular, familiar, famous

Paragraph 23

An **Incredible** Neighbor

My neighbor, Mrs. Wills, is an **amazing** person. She is 96 years old. My grandmother lived to be 87. Mrs. Wills lives alone, and she takes care of herself. In the morning, she works in her beautiful garden. She also does all of her own cooking. She does not like to cook rice. She cleans her own house. She even puts her heavy garbage can by the street for trash collection. She pulls the can slowly to the **curb**, and she goes up and down the steps to her door by herself. I hope to have that much energy and ability when I am 96 years old.

incredible: difficult to believe, amazing, surprising
amazing: remarkable; wonderful
curb: side of the street

Paragraph 24

My Office

My office is a comfortable place to work. On the left side of the room, there is a big **wooden** desk. My computer sits on top of the desk, and the printer sits under the desk. I keep paper **files** in the drawers. On the right side of the room, there are two beautiful bookcases. My father makes bookcases and other wood furniture. These bookcases are full of books, magazines, and computer software. There is also a telephone and a fax machine in my office. I have trouble remembering my fax number. There is a closet next to the fax machine. All my office supplies are there. I enjoy my office very much.

wooden: made of wood   **files:** documents; papers

WRITER'S NOTE: Check for the Verb

Do you sometimes forget to include the verb in a sentence? Many writers make this mistake. This is the rule: Every sentence needs a verb.

Incorrect: My father's name Samuel.
Correct: My father's name is Samuel.

Incorrect:	Many people in Switzerland French.
Correct:	Many people in Switzerland speak French.
Incorrect:	Some elementary schools computers for the students.
Correct:	Some elementary schools have computers for the students.

When you check your writing, look at each sentence carefully. Is there a verb? Remember that every sentence needs a verb.

Editing

 **Activity 13** | **Editing: Checking for Verbs**

On the Web
Try Unit 2
Activity 7

Read this paragraph. Five sentences are missing the verb be. *Find these five sentences and then add the correct form of the* be *verb. The first one is done for you.*

Paragraph 25

Staying Healthy

    is
It ˄ easy to stay healthy if you **follow** some simple steps. First, think about the food you eat. The best types of food fruits and vegetables. It important to eat a lot of them every day. Next, **consider** some exercise. Doctors say that one hour of **moderate** exercise each day can keep you in good shape. In addition, exercise good for the body and the mind. Finally, relaxation very important. Take time to **appreciate** the good things in life. You can follow these steps to help yourself stay healthy.

follow: obey; do
steps: directions
consider: think about
moderate: an average amount
appreciate: enjoy

WORKING WITH CONCLUDING SENTENCES

You learned about topic sentences and supporting sentences. All good paragraphs have a topic sentence. The topic sentence is usually (but not always) the first sentence in a paragraph. The body of a paragraph contains several supporting sentences. These sentences must relate to the topic sentence.

A paragraph may end with another part called the concluding sentence. The concluding sentence often gives a summary of the information in the paragraph. In many cases, the information in the topic sentence is similar to the information in the concluding sentence.

Look at the topic sentences and concluding sentences from these paragraphs in this unit.

	Paragraph 5, Page 41	**Paragraph 6, Page 43**	**Paragraph 7, Page 44**
Topic Sentence	I have a dream to visit Alaska.	It is obvious that my favorite color is blue.	I work in a popular building called the Franklin Building.
Concluding Sentence	I hope to visit this wonderful state soon.	Other colors are nice, but I like blue the best.	Everyone likes the Franklin Building very much.

Activity 14   **Concluding Sentences**

Copy the topic sentence and the concluding sentence from each paragraph indicated. How are the two sentences the same? How are they different? Discuss with a partner.

1. Paragraph 10, p. 49

   Topic sentence: _____

   Concluding sentence: _____

2. Paragraph 11, p. 49

   Topic sentence: _____

   Concluding sentence: _____

3. Paragraph 12, p. 50

   Topic sentence: _____

   Concluding sentence: _____

4. Paragraph 13, p. 50

Topic sentence: _____

Concluding sentence: _____

5. Paragraph 14, p. 51

Topic sentence: _____

Concluding sentence: _____

6. Paragraph 15, p. 51

Topic sentence: _____

Concluding sentence: _____

Activity 15   **Choosing Concluding Sentences**

Read each paragraph. Then read the concluding sentences below it. Circle the letter of the best concluding sentence.

Paragraph 26

Monday

I hate Monday for many reasons. One reason is work. I get up early to go to work on Monday. After a weekend of fun and relaxation, I don't like to go to work. Another reason that I don't like Monday is that I have three meetings every Monday. These meetings last a long time, and they are **extremely** boring. Traffic is also a big problem on Monday. There are more cars on the road on Monday. Drivers are in a bad **mood**, and I must be more careful than usual.

extremely: very   mood: disposition; humor

    a. Monday is worse than Tuesday, but it is better than Sunday.

    b. I don't like meetings on Monday.

    c. These are just a few reasons why I don't like Monday.

Paragraph 27

Good Luck, Bad Luck

Superstitions can mean good luck or bad luck. For example, some people believe that the number 7 is lucky. Other people think that if you see a shooting star, you can make a wish and it will come true. However, most superstitions are bad luck. **For instance**, many people believe that it is bad luck to open an umbrella inside a house. They also think that it is bad luck if a black cat walks in front of you. Other people think that if your left ear is burning, someone is saying something bad about you.

for instance: for example

    a. People believe exactly the same superstitions.

    b. It is amazing how many good and bad superstitions there are!

    c. The worst superstition is about breaking a mirror.

Paragraph 28

Buying a Car

Buying a car **requires** careful planning. Do you want a new or a used car? This depends on how much money you can spend. Sometimes a used car needs repairs. What style of car do you want? You can look at many different models to help you decide. Next, do you want extra **features** in your new car? Adding lots of extra features makes a car more expensive. Finally, you have to decide where you will buy your car.

requires: needs   features: options, such as air-conditioning or tinted windows

    a. It is important to think about all these things when you are buying a car.

    b. The most important thing is the kind of car that you want to buy.

    c. Will you buy your new car from a friend or a car dealer?

Editing

Activity 16 — **Editing: Grammar and Sentence Review**

Read this paragraph. There are seven mistakes: three (3) mistakes with adjectives, two (2) missing be verbs, and two (2) capitalization mistakes. Find and correct the mistakes.

Paragraph 29

Aspirin

aspirin is an incredible medicine. This small white pill is not a drug new. We do not know

exactly why or how it works. However, millions of people use aspirin every day. we take aspirin

for reasons many. Aspirin good for headaches, colds, and pain. Aspirin can help with so many

different health problems. Aspirin is a medicine simple, but it great.

Word Build•ing (wûrd bĭl'dĭng) n.

Activity 17　　**Word Building**

Study the following word forms. For the sentences on the right, choose the best word and write it in the blank space. Be sure to use the correct form of the verb. (Note: The word in bold is the original word that appears in the unit.)

Noun	Verb	Adjective	Sentence Practice
dream	dream	Ø	1. She _____ about becoming a famous singer.
			2. My _____ is to travel to India.
love	**love**	love**ly**	3. Your dress is _____.
			4. Mario and Yumiko _____ hip-hop music.
problem	Ø	problem**atic**	5. There is a _____ with my car's air conditioning.
			6. The economic situation is _____.
enjoy**ment**	**enjoy**	enjoy**able**	7. The live music is here for everyone's _____.
			8. We always have an _____ time on vacation.
patience	Ø	**patient**	9. Good teachers have a lot of _____.
			10. My mother is a very _____ woman.

Noun endings:　　**-ment**
Adjective endings:　-ly, -atic, -able

Building Better Sentences

Correct and varied sentence structure is essential to the quality of your writing. For further practice, go to Practice 2 on page 237 in Appendix 16.

Activity 18 **Original Writing Practice**

Answer the following questions and write eight to ten sentences about travel. Copy your sentences into a paragraph below. Then use the checklist that follows. Put a check (✓) next to each step as you complete it.

Topic: Travel

1. What city do you want to visit? _____

2. What kind of transportation do you need to get to this city? _____

_____

3. What are some reasons to go there? Think of at least three reasons. (Use adjectives in your descriptions.)

    a. Reason 1: _____

    _____

    b. Reason 2: _____

    _____

    c. Reason 3: _____

    _____

4. List two or three special activities that you can do in this city.

    a. Activity 1: _____

    _____

    b. Activity 2: _____

    _____

    c. Activity 3 (optional): _____

    _____

5. How long do you want to stay in this city? _____

_____

6. Are you looking forward to visiting this city? (Answer in a complete sentence.) _____

_____

_____

Checklist

✔1. ❑ Use adjectives to describe this city.

✔2. ❑ Indent the first line of your paragraph.

✔3. ❑ Check the first sentence (topic sentence) and the last sentence (concluding sentence). Are they similar in meaning?

✔4. ❑ Check each sentence in your paragraph. Is every sentence related to your topic?

Paragraph 30

_____

_____

_____

_____

_____

_____

_____

_____

_____

Activity 19   **Peer Editing**

Exchange papers from Activity 18 with another student. Read your partner's paragraph. Use Peer Editing Sheet 2 on page 255 to help you talk about your partner's work.

Activity 20   **Journal Writing**

EXTRA WRITING

Here are ten ideas for journal writing. Write about as many as you can. Follow your teacher's directions. (We recommend that you skip a line after each line that you write. This gives your teacher a place to write comments.)

1. Write about New York City. What do you know about it? Do you want to visit this city? Why or why not?

2. Write about swimming or another sport. Do you like to practice this sport? How often? Why do you enjoy this sport?

3. Write about your favorite kind of music. Why do you like this music? How do you feel when you listen to this music?

4. Write about how to use a _____ . Explain the steps involved in using this item.

5. Write about credit cards. What is your opinion about them? Are they helpful or dangerous? Do you use them?

6. Write about a good weekend plan. What do you like to do on weekends? Who do you spend your weekends with?

7. Choose a person in your class to write about. Explain how the person looks and what his or her personality is like.

8. Write about a famous person you like. Who is this person? What is this person's job? Why do you like this person?

9. Write about something that you do not like. Give three reasons why you do not like this thing.

10. Write about your favorite subject in school. Why do you like this subject? What kinds of things do you practice in this subject?

MORE WRITING

For extra writing practice, see the activities in Unit 8, Appendix 17, and the *Great Sentences* website: http://esl.college.hmco.com/students.

Writing About the Present

UNIT 3

GOAL: To learn how to write sentences in the simple present tense

GRAMMAR AND SENTENCE STRUCTURE: Simple present tense; object pronouns; *a* and *an*

SENTENCE DEVELOPMENT: Compound sentences

BEGIN WITH THE PRESENT TENSE

When you write about daily habits and activities or things that are generally true, use the present tense.

GRAMMAR AND SENTENCE STRUCTURE: Simple Present Tense: Statements and Questions

In English, the present tense can be divided into two categories: regular verbs and the verbs *be* and *have*. Do you know the following verb forms?

Present Tense Verb Forms: Statements

Verb *be*	I **am**	we **are**
	you **are**	you (plural) **are**
	he / she / it **is**	they **are**

Verb *have*	I **have**	we **have**
	you **have**	you (plural) **have**
	he / she / it **has**	they **have**
Verb *live*	I **live**	we **live**
(regular)	you **live**	you (plural) **live**
	he / she / it **lives**	they **live**
Verb *go*	I **go**	we **go**
(regular)	you **go**	you (plural) **go**
	he / she / it **goes**	they **go**

Present Tense Verb Forms: Questions

Verb *be*	**Am** I . . . ?	**Are** we . . . ?
	Are you . . . ?	**Are** you (plural) . . . ?
	Is he / she / it . . . ?	**Are** they . . . ?
Verb *have*	**Do** I **have** . . . ?	**Do** we **have** . . . ?
	Do you **have** . . . ?	**Do** you (plural) **have** . . . ?
	Does he / she / it **have** . . . ?	**Do** they **have** . . . ?
Verb *live*	**Do** I **live** . . . ?	**Do** we **live** . . . ?
	Do you **live** . . . ?	**Do** you (plural) **live** . . . ?
	Does he / she / it **live** . . . ?	**Do** they **live** . . . ?
Verb *go*	**Do** I **go** . . . ?	**Do** we **go** . . . ?
	Do you **go** . . . ?	**Do** you (plural) **go** . . . ?
	Does he / she / it **go** . . . ?	**Do** they **go** . . . ?

WWW

**On the Web
Try Unit 3
Activity 5**

NOTE: All verbs except *be* must add *do* or *does* to make a question.

In this unit, you will practice writing sentences and paragraphs in the present tense.

WRITER'S NOTE: Using Contractions

A **contraction** is a short version of a pronoun and a verb combined, such as *I am / I'm*. The apostrophe (') shows where a letter has been left out. Here are some common contractions with *be*:

I am = I'm	we are = we're
you are = you're	you (plural) are = you're
he is = he's / she is = she's / it is = it's	they are = they're

Some instructors believe contractions are too informal for academic writing. Be sure to ask your instructor if using contractions is acceptable.

Activity 1   **Present Tense Forms**

Read each sentence. Write the correct form of the verb in parentheses.

On the Web Try Unit 3 Activity 1

Paragraph 31

Uncle Charlie

My Uncle Charlie (**1.** be) _____ a wonderful man. He (**2.** be)

_____ an entrepreneur. He began his restaurant business ten years ago. Now he

enjoys great success. In his restaurant, he (**3.** have) _____ ten waiters, two

managers, and three chefs. Uncle Charlie (**4.** work) _____ very hard in his

restaurant. Sometimes he is there seven days a week. He and his wife Valerie always (**5.** go)

_____ to the restaurant at night to make sure that the customers are happy. I (**6.**

love) _____ Uncle Charlie and Aunt Valerie, and I really appreciate all their hard

work. (**7.** You / know) _____ somebody like my uncle?

entrepreneur: a person who owns his/her own business

Activity 2   **The Verb *Be* in the Present**

Read this paragraph from Giacomo to his new classmate. Fill in the missing be verbs.

Paragraph 32

My Classmates

My classmates come from all over the world. José (**1.**) _____ from Spain, so

he speaks Spanish perfectly. Kuniko and Yasuhiro (**2.**) _____ Japanese, but they

don't sit next to each other in class. Yuri (**3.**) _____ from Ukraine, and he plays

soccer very well. The Al-Ahmad brothers (**4.**) _____ from Saudi Arabia, and they

(**5.**) _____ both very nice. Me? I (**6.**) _____ from Italy, and I love to

sing in class. We (**7.**) _____ all very good friends, and I hope we can be friends

forever. Where (**8.**) _____ you from?

Activity 3   **Verbs: Changing Singular to Plural**

Read the following paragraph. Make the following changes and rewrite the paragraph on the lines.

1. *Change the subject of the story, Jim, to Jim and Billy.*
2. *You will have to make certain changes to the verb forms and to some nouns and pronouns, too.*

On the Web
Try Unit 3
Activity 4

Paragraph 33

Jim's Daily Routine

EXAMPLE PARAGRAPH

Jim is a very busy student. He studies engineering at City College. Every day he wakes up at 7:00 in the morning, takes a shower, and then rushes off to school. He goes to school for six hours. After school, he goes to the local mall where he works in a sporting goods store. After this part-time job, he goes home, eats a quick dinner, studies, and does his homework. Jim knows that this lifestyle is stressful. He also knows that it will end soon, and he will get a professional job.

Jim and Billy's Daily Routine

Jim and Billy are very busy students.

_____

_____

_____

_____

_____

_____

_____

_____

_____

_____

_____

_____

_____

_____

_____

_____

| Activity 4 | **Writing a Paragraph from Pictures** |

Study the following pictures. They tell a story. Then read the incomplete paragraph. Some present tense verbs are missing. Fill in the blanks based on the pictures. Write the full sentence for the last two sentences. Note: The numbers in the paragraph correspond to the pictures.

Paragraph 34

One Family's Morning Routine

The Lee family is very busy on weekday mornings. (**1.**) Every morning Susan Lee, the youngest daughter, wakes up and _____ for her parents and siblings. She loves to cook! (**2.**) When breakfast is ready, the rest of the family _____ . The kids eat breakfast quickly. (**3.**) After they eat, Susan's father and mother _____ . (**4.**) At 8:30 A.M., Mr. Lee _____ (**5.**) Then he and the kids _____ to Mrs. Lee. (**6.**) Mr. Lee and the kids _____ the **minivan** so that he can take them to school. (**7.**) _____ . (**8.**) A few minutes later, _____ .

siblings: brothers and/or sisters   **minivan:** a large family car, usually with sliding doors

Editing

Activity 5   **Editing: Subjects and Verbs**

Read the following paragraph. There are seven errors. Most of the sentences are missing either the subject or the verb. Write the corrections above the errors. The first one has been done for you.

Paragraph 35

The City of Budapest

             is

Budapest ∧ one of the most interesting capitals of Europe. Is a romantic city, and it has many

interesting tourist places to visit. One example the Danube River. It separates Budapest into

Buda and Pest. In addition, visitors Hungarian traditional food. The most popular food goulash

soup. The people of Budapest friendly and helpful to tourists. When travel to Europe, you can

visit Budapest and have a very good time.

WRITER'S NOTE:
Review of *There Is* and *There Are*

- The expressions *there is* and *there are* come at the beginning of a sentence to show that something exists in a certain place.
- Follow *there is* with a singular noun.
- Follow *there are* with a plural noun.
- You must use the word *there* in this kind of sentence.
- Writers often use *there is* and *there are* with a place phrase.

Look at the following examples.

Incorrect:	There is ten people in my office.
Correct:	There are ten people in my office.
Incorrect:	Is a cat in the room.
Correct:	There is a cat in the room.
Incorrect:	Are apples on the table.
Correct:	There are apples on the table.
Incorrect:	A concert at the university tomorrow.
Correct:	There is a concert at the university tomorrow.

(Note: For an introduction to there is and there are, see p. 22 in Unit 1.)

Activity 6	Practicing *There Is / There Are*

Read this paragraph about a classroom. Study the four examples of there is *and* there are *in the paragraph and answer the questions.*

Paragraph 36

A Description of My Classroom

My classroom is a very colorful room. (**1**) *There are* twenty desks in the room. Each desk has a dark brown seat and a shiny white top. On the left side of the room, (**2**) *there is* a world map. This map shows all the different countries in the world, and each country is a different color. On the right side of the room, (**3**) *there are* two posters. The first poster is green. It has a list of fifty common verbs. The second poster has the names and pictures of fruits and vegetables. It is white, but the writing is black. Finally, (**4**) *there are* some pictures of wild animals above the blackboard. These objects make my classroom colorful.

a. Is (1) singular or plural? _____ Why? _____

b. Is (2) singular or plural? _____ Why? _____

c. Is (3) singular or plural? _____ Why? _____

d. Is (4) singular or plural? _____ Why? _____

e. Is there a map in the room? _____ Where? _____

f. Is there a calendar in the room? _____ Where? _____

g. Is there a cat in the room? _____ Where? _____

h. Are there animal pictures in the room? _____ Where? _____

| Activity 7 | **Using *There Is / There Are*** |

Look at the picture of the living room. On the lines, write seven sentences about the objects in the picture. Use there is *and* there are.

1. _____

2. _____

3. _____

4. _____

5. _____

6. _____

7. _____

Activity 8 **Find the Errors**

Read this paragraph about the English alphabet. Find the four mistakes. Circle the mistakes and correct them. On the lines, explain your corrections.

Paragraph 37

The English Alphabet

There have twenty-six letters in the English alphabet. There is five vowel letters and twenty-one consonant letters. The five vowels are *a, e, i, o,* and *u.* The letters *w* and *y* is sometimes vowels, especially when they come after vowels. Three letters have the *a* sound in them. These letters is *a, j,* and *k.* Nine letters have the *e* sound in them. These are *b, c, d, e, g, p, t, v,* and *z.* If you want to speak English well, you have to learn the twenty-six letters of the English alphabet.

1. _____

2. _____

3. _____

4. _____

Editing

Activity 9 **Editing: Capitalization Review**

You studied capitalization in Unit 1. Read the following paragraph about the TOEFL exam. There are ten errors in capitalization. Can you find them all? Circle the capitalization errors and write the corrections above the circled words. The first one has been done for you.

Paragraph 38

The TOEFL

Do you know about the TOEFL? It is the Test of English as a Foreign Language. Most international students who want to study at a university in the (united) states take this test. it measures english language ability. The test comes from Educational Testing Service in new jersey. It is a very long test. the computer version of the TOEFL contains four tasks: Listening

Comprehension, Structure, Reading Comprehension, and Essay Writing. if you want to study in

the united states, it is important to prepare for this test and get a high score.

NEGATIVES AND THE PRESENT TENSE

Good writers can use the negative form of the present tense. This section gives you practice with negatives.

GRAMMAR AND SENTENCE STRUCTURE:
Present Tense Verb Forms: Negatives

Verb *be*   I am <u>not</u>   we **are** <u>not</u>

            you **are** <u>not</u>   you (plural) **are** <u>not</u>

            he / she / it **is** <u>not</u>   they **are** <u>not</u>

NOTE: Some contractions are possible with the verb *be* in negative forms.

   is not = isn't   are not = aren't

Verb *have*   I <u>**do not**</u> have   we <u>**do not**</u> have

            you <u>**do not**</u> have   you (plural) <u>**do not**</u> have

            he / she / it <u>**does not**</u> have   they <u>**do not**</u> have

Verb *live*   I <u>**do not**</u> live   we <u>**do not**</u> live

            you <u>**do not**</u> live   you (plural) <u>**do not**</u> live

            he / she / it <u>**does not**</u> live   they <u>**do not**</u> live

Verb *go*   I <u>**do not**</u> go   we <u>**do not**</u> go

            you <u>**do not**</u> go   you (plural) <u>**do not**</u> go

            he / she / it <u>**does not**</u> go   they <u>**do not**</u> go

there is / there are   there isn't   there aren't

NOTE: Contractions are possible with negative forms of regular verbs.

   do not go = don't go   does not go = doesn't go

**On the Web
Try Unit 3
Activity 2**

Activity 10 | **Affirmative and Negative**

Read the sentences. Change the verb from the positive to the negative. Also write the contraction form. The first one has been done for you.

1. I have (contraction) a car. _I do not (OR don't) have a car._ _____

2. New York City is in California. _____

3. The capital of Japan is Osaka. _____

4. George goes to the library every day. _____

5. There is a Thai restaurant on Green Street. _____

6. Irene and Julie are roommates. _____

7. Charlie works at a gas station. _____

8. There are answers in the back of the book. _____

9. The teacher wants a new computer. _____

10. Alice bakes cookies often. _____

SENTENCES WITH OBJECT PRONOUNS

In Unit 2 you studied subject pronouns. Object pronouns have different forms that you need to learn.

GRAMMAR AND SENTENCE STRUCTURE: Object Pronouns

You learned that a pronoun is a word that takes the place of a noun.

After Verbs

An object pronoun usually comes after a verb. In English, there are seven object pronouns.

Singular	Plural
me	us
you	you
him / her / it	them

Examples:

Singular	**Plural**
Mona likes <u>me</u>.	Mona likes <u>us</u>.
Do I know <u>you</u>?	Do I know <u>you</u>?
Karen doesn't understand <u>him</u>.	Karen doesn't understand <u>them</u>.

After Prepositions

An **object pronoun** can also come after a preposition. A **preposition** is a word that shows location, time, or direction. Some common prepositions are *to*, *with*, and *at*. Other prepositions include: *on*, *in*, *for*, *by*, *near*, *under*, *from*.

Examples:

Singular	**Plural**
Assad walks with <u>me</u>.	Assad walks with <u>us</u>.
Can I give the message to <u>you</u>?	Can I give the message to <u>you</u>?
Jane listens to <u>him</u>.	Jane listens to <u>them</u>.

Activity 11 — Object Pronouns

Read the following paragraph. Replace the proper nouns in parentheses with an object pronoun. The first one has been done for you.

Paragraph 39

My Best Friend

My best friend is Gretchen. I met (**1.** Gretchen) <u>her</u> ten years ago. She is from Alabama.

She comes from a very large family. She has four brothers and three sisters. She doesn't live with

(**2.** her brothers and sisters) _____ . They live in Alabama with their parents.

Gretchen studies veterinary medicine at the University of Florida in Gainesville. She loves

(**3.** Gainesville) _____ very much. She also enjoys animals. Gretchen has three

pets. She has a cat. She also has a small dog. Gretchen's third pet is a large boa constrictor.

She likes (**4.** her pets) _____ all very much. In her free time, Gretchen plays tennis,

reads books, and cooks gourmet meals. I love (**5.** Gretchen) _____ like a sister. I

hope that our friendship will stay with (**6.** Gretchen and me) _____ for many years.

| Activity 12 | Possessive Adjective Review: Interviewing a Classmate |

Find out the answers to these questions. Ask your classmate. Then write down the answers. Try to use possessive pronouns. Follow the example.

Example:

What is your classmate's name? His name is Alberto.

1. What is your classmate's name? _____

2. Where is your classmate from? _____

3. How big is your classmate's family? _____

4. Why is your classmate in this class? _____

5. What job does your classmate want to do in the future? _____

_____

| Activity 13 | Writing Information in Paragraph Form |

Write the information about your classmate (from Activity 12) in the form of a paragraph. If you need some help in organization, review Paragraph 39 in Activity 11.

_____

_____

_____

_____

_____

_____

_____

_____

SENTENCE TYPES: SIMPLE AND COMPOUND

All the sentences you have written in the activities up to now have been simple sentences. As you learned in Unit 1, a simple sentence has a subject and a verb. Good writers often combine two simple sentences into one longer sentence. The longer sentence is called a compound sentence.

Simple and Compound Sentences

On the Web
Try Unit 3
Activity 3
and
Activity 6

Simple Sentences

A simple sentence usually has one subject and one verb.

<u>Japan</u> <u>imports</u> oil from Saudi Arabia.

However, a simple sentence can have more than one subject and more than one verb in these combinations:

2 subjects + 1 verb: <u>Japan</u> and <u>Germany</u> <u>import</u> oil from Saudi Arabia.
                SUBJECTS + VERB

1 subject + 2 verbs: <u>Japan</u> <u>imports</u> oil and <u>exports</u> cars.
           SUBJECT + VERBS

2 subjects + 2 verbs: <u>Japan</u> and <u>Germany</u> <u>import</u> oil and <u>export</u> cars.
               SUBJECTS + VERBS

Notice that all of these sentences have one basic subject-verb combination.

Compound Sentences

A compound sentence is two sentences joined by a connecting word, such as *and, but,* or *so.* A compound sentence has two subjects and two verbs:

<u>Japan</u> <u>imports</u> oil, and <u>Saudi Arabia</u> <u>imports</u> vegetables.
SUBJECT #1 + VERB #1   SUBJECT #2 + VERB #2

<u>Sue</u> <u>watched</u> TV, and <u>Ben</u> <u>wrote</u> letters.
SUBJECT #1 + VERB #1   SUBJECT #2 + VERB #2

NOTE: Compound sentences *always* use a comma (,) and a connecting word (*and, but, so*) to connect two sentences.

SENTENCE DEVELOPMENT

SENTENCE DEVELOPMENT

Activity 14 Sentence Types

Read each sentence. Write S or C to label it as simple or compound. The first two have been done for you. Hint: Look for the connectors and, but, *or* so *in compound sentences.*

1. __C__ Japan's flag is red and white, and the Canadian flag is also red and white.

2. __S__ Japan and Canada have the same two colors in their flags.

3. _____ The weather is bad, so the plane cannot take off on time.

4. _____ It is extremely hot in this room without an air conditioner.

5. _____ This map does not include the newly independent countries in Europe or Asia.

6. _____ For less than two hundred dollars, you can buy a round-trip ticket to Boston.

7. _____ The students take a test every Friday, but their scores are not very high.

8. _____ January, March, May, July, August, October, and December have thirty-one days.

9. _____ This recipe requires two cups of flour, two cups of sugar, and one cup of milk.

10. _____ Each ring costs sixty dollars, so five rings cost three hundred dollars.

11. _____ Some people prefer silver rings, but most people prefer gold rings.

12. _____ These silver and gold rings are different in weight and in price.

Activity 15 Simple Sentences to Compound Sentences

Read each pair of simple sentences. Combine them into one sentence with a comma and a connecting word. Write the compound sentence on the line.

1. Mary lives in Turkey. Abdul lives in Kuwait. (but)

_____

2. The weather was cold. I stayed indoors. (so)

_____

3. We go to school every day. We play tennis on weekends. (and)

_____

4. Linus and Kathy are related. They are not brother and sister. (but)

_____

5. The restaurant manager was happy. He gave all the servers a raise. (so)

_____

WRITER'S NOTE: Brainstorming *Why* Questions

You use the word *because* to answer a question with *why*. You can put *because* at the beginning or in the middle of a sentence. If you use it at the beginning of a sentence, follow this clause with a comma. *Because* is never used in a simple sentence.

> *Because* Laura felt ill, she went to the doctor.
>
> Laura went to the doctor *because* she felt ill.
>
> Ian ate dinner *because* he was hungry.

(NOTE: See page 151 for more information on *because*.)

WRITER'S NOTE: Brainstorming with Questions

When you write a paragraph, sometimes it is difficult to find enough information to include. Good writers often ask questions to help them get ideas about what to write. First, think about your topic. Then imagine someone who does not know much about the topic. What questions might that person ask?

Quickly write down as many questions about the topic as you can think of. Don't worry now whether the questions sound good. Your purpose is just to make a list of questions. Later you can go back and read the questions. Then you can decide which questions are good ideas to write about.

Example:

> *Topic:* Writing about a popular sport

Possible questions:

1. What is a popular sport?
2. Why is it popular?
3. How many people are needed to play this sport?
4. Is the sport difficult to learn?
5. Where (in which countries) is the sport popular?
6. Is this sport popular on television?

7. How much training does someone need in this sport?

8. How old is this sport?

9. Do you need a lot of equipment to play this sport?

10. Is there a worldwide competition in this sport?

Can you think of other questions?

11. _____

12. _____

Activity 16	Questions and a Paragraph About Soccer

The following paragraph about soccer answers some of the questions from the Writer's Note: Brainstorming with Questions. Review the soccer questions and read the paragraph. On the lines below, write the questions that the writer used to create the paragraph.

Paragraph 40

EXAMPLE PARAGRAPH

A Popular Sport

The sport of soccer is the most popular athletic activity in the world. Many people believe that this game comes from England, but others believe that it comes from the Etruscans (a group of people who lived in what is now known as Tuscany in Italy). Soccer is an international phenomenon. People all over the world play and follow this sport. Soccer is popular because it is cheap and fun. It does not require special equipment. It is also fun to watch on television. Every four years, the world enjoys watching the World Cup soccer championship. This time is probably the most exciting time for soccer teams and their fans.

Refer to pages 84–85 for the list of questions:

_____

_____

_____

_____

_____

_____

_____

_____

_____

_____

_____

_____

GRAMMAR AND SENTENCE STRUCTURE:
Using *A* and *An* with Count Nouns

A count noun is a noun that you can count. A count noun has a singular form and a plural form. A noncount noun has only one form.

If you have a singular count noun, use *a* or *an* in front of that noun when it is general (not specific). Use *a* in front of a singular count noun that begins with a consonant sound. Use *an* in front of a singular count noun that begins with a vowel sound.

Forgetting to put *a* or *an* in front of a count noun is a grammatical error. (You will learn more about indefinite articles in Unit 6, p. 147.)

NONCOUNT	COUNT	
	<u>Singular</u>	<u>Plural</u>
money	a dollar	twenty dollars
ice	an ice cube	ice cubes
information	a number	numbers
clothing	a blue shirt	blue shirts
vocabulary	a word	fifteen words
bread	a slice of bread	slices of bread
honesty	an honest person	honest people
homework	an assignment	three assignments

Activity 17   **Count and Noncount Words**

Look at the words listed below. On the line to the left, write C if the word is count and NC if the word is noncount. Then circle all words that can be used in this blank: This is _____ . The first two have been done for you.

1. __C__   (a cat)   cats   a cats   cat

2. __NC__   a ice   an ice   (ice)   ices

3. _____   moneys   a money   money   a moneys

4. _____   bread   breads   a breads   a bread

5. _____   an eraser   a eraser   erasers   an erasers

6. _____   homeworks   a homework   a homeworks   homework

7. _____   an unit   units   a unit   an units

8. _____   a country   country   an country   a countries

9. _____   information   informations   an information   a information

10. _____   happiness   a happiness   happinesses   an happiness

11. _____   word   a word   words   a words

12. _____   an present   a presents   presents   a present

13. _____   a answer   answers   an answers   an answer

14. _____   politician   politicians   a politician   a politicians

Editing

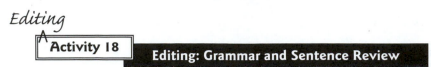

Activity 18   **Editing: Grammar and Sentence Review**

Read this paragraph. There are ten errors: two (2) errors with verbs, one (1) punctuation error, two (2) capitalization errors, two (2) adjective errors, two (2) possessive adjective errors, and one (1) subject pronoun error. Find and correct the errors. The first one has been done for you.

Paragraph 41

Not an Average Teenager

Steven Mills is not a typical teenager. Steven is a gymnast, and he ~~want~~ wants to compete in the

olympics. He wakes up at five o'clock in the morning every day, because he has to practice before

school. First, he has a breakfast healthy. Then she jogs to National Gymnasium on Cypress street.

He practices gymnastics for two hours. Then he gets ready for school. Steven goes to school from

eight-thirty in the morning until three o'clock in the afternoon. After school, he returns to the

gymnasium for classes special with him coach. When practice finish at six o'clock, Steven returns

home. He eats dinner, does his homework, and talks with their family. Steven is in bed by ten

o'clock, so he will be ready for work the next day.

Word Build•ing (wûrd bĭl'dĭng) *n.*

Activity 19   **Word Building**

Study the following word forms. For the sentences on the right, choose the best word and write it in the blank space. Be sure to use the correct form of the verb. (Note: The word in bold is the original word that appears in the unit.)

Noun	Verb	Adjective	Sentence Practice
friend/friend<u>ship</u>	Ø	friend<u>ly</u>	1. My best _____ lives in Mexico.
			2. It is important to be _____ to others.

profession/professional (A THING)/ (A PERSON)	Ø	professio<u>nal</u>	3. Computer graphics is a popular _____.
			4. Her _____ experience is impressive.
separa<u>tion</u>	separate	**separate**	5. I _____ my clothes before washing them.
			6. Joann and her husband drive _____ cars.
visitor/visit (A PERSON)/ (A THING)	visit	Ø	7. Wake up! There is a _____ waiting to see you.
			8. Every Sunday, Maria _____ her sister.
free<u>dom</u>	free	**free**	9. In college, you have the _____ to choose your major.
			10. There is a _____ movie playing tonight.

Noun endings: -ship, -dom, -al
Adjective endings: -al, -ly

Building Better Sentences

Correct and varied sentence structure is essential to the quality of your writing.
For further practice, go to Practice 3 on page 237 in Appendix 16.

Activity 20   **Original Writing Practice**

Write a paragraph about a sport you enjoy. In your paragraph, answer the questions below. Can you think of more questions? Then use the checklist in the box below. Put a check (✓) next to each step as you complete it.

1. Which sport do you enjoy?

2. Why do you like this sport?

3. Do you play this sport? If so, how often?

4. Is the sport difficult to learn?

5. Do you like a particular athlete (or team) in this sport? Why?

Checklist

✔1. ❑ Make sure every sentence has a subject and a verb.

✔2. ❑ Make sure the verbs are in the correct tense.

✔3. ❑ Make sure every sentence begins with a capital letter.

✔4. ❑ Make sure that all the proper nouns (names, cities, countries, etc.) are capitalized.

✔5. ❑ Make sure every sentence ends with the correct punctuation.

✔6. ❑ Create a title for your paragraph.

Activity 21   **Peer Editing**

Choose someone that you work well with. Exchange papers from Activity 20 with that student. Read your partner's paragraph. Use Peer Editing Sheet 3 on page 257 to help you talk about your partner's work.

Activity 22   **Journal Writing**

EXTRA WRITING

Here are ten ideas for journal writing. Choose one or more of them to write about. Follow your teacher's directions. (We recommend that you skip a line after each line that you write. This gives your teacher a place to write comments.)

1. Choose a member of your family. Write a paragraph about this person. Include the person's name, age, nationality, job, hobbies, etc.

2. Write about your typical routine for a day of the week. Include the time that you usually wake up, what you eat for breakfast, what your activities are during the day, whom you spend your time with, how you enjoy the day, and what time you go to bed.

3. Write about a special city in a particular country. Include the name of the city, the population, the special tourist attractions, and why it is an important city for you.

4. Write about a job that interests you. Include the title of the job, the duties of the job, and why it is interesting to you.

5. What is your favorite web site? Write about a web site that you like. What is the address? What kind of information does it have? Why do you like it?

6. Write about your best friend. What is his/her name? Where does he/she live? What makes your friendship special?

7. Write about a restaurant that you like. What is the name of this restaurant? Why do you like it? What kind of food does it serve? What is the price range? How is it decorated?

8. Write about your favorite movie. What is the title? Who are the main actors in the movie? What is the story about? Why do you like this movie?

9. Write about a specific food that you know how to cook. What are the ingredients? Is it easy to prepare? Are the ingredients expensive?

10. Write about a type of music that you *do not* enjoy. Why don't you like it? How does it make you feel when you hear it?

MORE WRITING

For extra writing practice, see the activities in Unit 8, Appendix 17, and the *Great Sentences* website: http://esl.college.hmco.com/students.

UNIT

4

Writing About the Past

GOAL: To learn how to write sentences in the past tense

GRAMMAR AND SENTENCE STRUCTURE: Past tense of *be* and regular verbs; forming questions; past tense of irregular verbs; forming the negative past tense of *be*; forming the negative past tense of other verbs

SENTENCE DEVELOPMENT: Compound sentences with *but*

BEGIN WITH THE PAST TENSE

What happened yesterday? What happened last week? When you talk about actions in the past, you use the simple past tense. Both regular verbs and irregular verbs can be in the simple past tense.

GRAMMAR AND SENTENCE STRUCTURE:
Simple Past Tense: Statements and Questions

Past Tense of Be

The most common verb in English, *be*, is an irregular verb. Study the simple past tense form of the verb *be*.

Verb *be*	I **was**	we **were**
	you **were**	you (plural) **were**
	he / she / it **was**	they **were**

To form questions with the verb *be* in past tense, use the forms on page 93.

Past Tense of *Be*: Questions

Verb *be*	**Was** I . . . ?	**Were** we . . . ?
	Were you . . . ?	**Were** you (plural) . . . ?
	Was he / she / it . . . ?	**Were** they . . . ?

Incorrect:	I am in Guatemala last year.
Incorrect:	I were in Guatemala last year.
Correct:	I was in Guatemala last year.
Incorrect:	Was Rachel and Mario at the mall yesterday?
Incorrect:	Rachel and Mario were at the mall yesterday?
Correct:	Were Rachel and Mario at the mall yesterday?

Past Tense of Regular Verbs

Forming the simple past of regular verbs is easy. Just add *-d* or *-ed* to the ends of regular verbs. (See Appendix 4 for more about the spelling of regular past tense verbs.) Study the examples below.

**On the Web
Try Unit 4
Activity 1**

Verb *live*	I **lived**	we **lived**
	you **lived**	you (plural) **lived**
	he / she / it **lived**	they **lived**
Verb *visit*	I **visited**	we **visited**
	you **visited**	you (plural) **visited**
	he / she / it **visited**	they **visited**

Past Tense of Regular Verbs: Questions

Verb *live*	**Did** I **live** . . . ?	**Did** we **live** . . . ?
	Did you **live** . . . ?	**Did** you (plural) **live** . . . ?
	Did he / she / it **live** . . . ?	**Did** they **live** . . . ?

NOTE: The question form of past tense verbs is easy to make. Just use *did* to show that the sentence is in *past* tense and that it is a *question*. The main verb in questions uses the simple (base) form: *did* + subject + *verb* (no *-ed*!).

Now study these sentences for correct forms of the past tense in statements and questions.

Incorrect:	We call our parents yesterday.
Correct:	We called our parents yesterday.
Incorrect:	Do the tourists hike down the mountain last night?
Incorrect:	The tourists hiked down the mountain last night?
Correct:	Did the tourists hike down the mountain last night?

WRITER'S NOTE: Time Phrases with Past Tense

We use certain words and phrases in a sentence to help show that something happened in the past. Some of these include:

last night   last week   this morning   yesterday   two minutes ago

You can put these time phrases at the beginning or the end of a sentence. Avoid using them in the middle of a sentence. Study these examples. Can you think of any others?

Incorrect:	I yesterday scratched my knee.
Correct:	Yesterday I scratched my knee.
Correct:	I scratched my knee yesterday.
Incorrect:	Did Maria last night go to the party?
Correct:	Did Maria go to the party last night?

**On the Web
Try Unit 4
Activity 2**

Activity 1   **Sentences with Past Tense**

The verbs in these sentences are in the present tense. Rewrite the sentences and change the verbs to the past tense. The first sentence has been done for you.

1. Mary and her daughter Natalie visit the farm.

    Mary and her daughter Natalie visited the farm.

2. Mary and Natalie play with many animals.

3. They laugh at the animals.

4. Natalie really enjoys herself.

5. She likes the chickens best.

6. Natalie watches them play all morning.

7. They play with the baby goats.

_____

8. Finally, they return home.

_____

| Activity 2 | **More Work with Past Tense**

Read the paragraph and circle the ten past tense verbs. When you finish, answer the questions in complete sentences. The first one has been done for you.

Paragraph 42

Lao-Tzu and Taoism

Lao-Tzu (was) a Chinese **philosopher**. He was born in China, and he lived in the Hunan **province**. Lao-Tzu worked as a court **librarian**. The government was **corrupt**, so Lao-Tzu decided to leave his home. Before he **abandoned** the province, someone asked him to write a book about how to live correctly. He agreed to write the book *Tao Te Ching*. It was the beginning of the philosophy of Taoism.

philosopher: a person who studies the universe, nature, life, and morals
province: a territory in a country
librarian: someone who works with books
corrupt: dishonest
abandoned: left (He left the province.)

Information for this paragraph came from *Microsoft Encarta 96* and *Simple Abundance: A Daybook of Comfort and Joy* by Sarah Ban Breathnach, published by Warner Books, Inc., 1995.

1. Who was Lao-Tzu?

   Lao-Tzu was a famous philosopher.

2. Where was he born?

   _____

3. What was his job?

   _____

4. What did he do before he left his home?

_____

5. What did this book create?

_____

| Activity 3 | An Important Person |

Think of an important person in the past. It could be someone famous in history. It could be a famous singer, politician, or athlete. It could be someone from your family. Answer the questions using complete sentences.

1. Who was this person?

_____

2. Where was the person born?

_____

3. What was the person's job?

_____

4. Why is the person important to you? What did he or she do?

_____

_____

_____

Editing

| Activity 4 | Editing: Plural to Singular |

Read the paragraph. Circle all of the past tense verbs. Then follow the directions and make changes to the paragraph. The first sentence has been done for you. (You may want to review subject pronouns and possessive adjectives in Unit 2.)

On the Web
Try Unit 4
Activity 3

Paragraph 43

The Top of the Class

In 1992, Anthony and Marcus (were) students at the University of North Carolina. <u>They</u> studied in the criminology department. <u>They</u> excelled in <u>their</u> studies. In class, <u>they</u> answered all of <u>their</u> instructors' questions. <u>Their</u> test grades beat the other students', and <u>their</u> class projects received excellent marks. When <u>they</u> graduated in 1996, <u>they</u> finished at the top of the class. All of the teachers were very proud of Anthony and Marcus.

Rewrite the paragraph on the lines below and make these changes:

1. Change *Anthony and Marcus* to *Marcia*. (Note: Marcia is a woman's name.)
2. Change the underlined pronouns to go with *Marcia*.
3. Change any other words necessary (such as *students* to *student* in the first sentence).

The Top of the Class

In 1992, Marcia was a student at the University of North Carolina.

_____

_____

_____

_____

_____

_____

_____

_____

_____

| Activity 5 | Answering Questions with *Be* |

First, discuss these questions with your classmates.

1. How do deaf people communicate with each other?
2. How do blind people read?
3. Do you know anyone who is both deaf and blind?

Then read the paragraph. Answer the questions below using forms of be. *Use complete sentences. The first one has been done for you.*

Paragraph 44

EXAMPLE PARAGRAPH

Helen Keller (1880–1968)

Helen Keller was a famous American author. She was born healthy. However, when she was two years old, she became very ill. The illness made her **deaf** and **blind**. She couldn't communicate with anyone. When she was seven years old, a teacher taught her how to communicate. The teacher's name was Annie Sullivan. When Helen was twenty years old, she started college. After her graduation, she wrote thirteen books and traveled around the world. She was an incredible woman.

deaf: not able to hear   **blind:** not able to see

1. What was the blind and deaf person's name?

    The blind and deaf person's name was Helen Keller.

2. What country was she from?

3. Was she healthy or unhealthy when she was born?

4. How old was she when she became ill?

5. Who was her teacher?

6. How old was she when she learned to communicate?

7. How old was she when she went to college?

_____

8. What did she do after graduation?

_____

IRREGULAR PAST TENSE VERBS

In this unit, you have learned how to make the past tense of a regular verb—add *-d* or *-ed* to the simple form of the verb. Some verbs, however, are irregular. This means that they take a different form in the past tense.

On the Web
Try Unit 4
Activity 4

GRAMMAR AND SENTENCE STRUCTURE:
Past Tense of Irregular Verbs

Here are some common irregular verbs. (See Appendix 5 for a complete list of common irregular past tense verbs.)

be	was/were	feel	felt	pay	paid	send	sent
buy	bought	go	went	run	ran	sit	sat
do	did	have	had	ride	rode	speak	spoke
draw	drew	leave	left	say	said	teach	taught
cut	cut	make	made	see	saw	write	wrote

NOTE: To form questions with irregular verbs, follow the rules for regular verbs on page 93. Use *did* and the simple (present tense) verb form.

There is no special rule that tells when a verb is irregular. You must memorize the past tense form when you learn the word. A dictionary will tell you when a verb is irregular. Now study these sentences for correct forms of the irregular past tense in statements and in questions.

Incorrect:	Last night I buy a new CD.
Incorrect:	Last night I buyed a new CD.
Correct:	Last night I bought a new CD.
Incorrect:	Did you left your dictionary at home?
Incorrect:	Do you left your dictionary at home?
Correct:	Did you leave your dictionary at home?

Activity 6	**Complete the Paragraph**

Read the paragraph. It is missing two sentences. Use the pictures to create a sentence for each blank. Be sure the paragraph makes sense.

Paragraph 45

A Surprising Day

Yesterday I decided to go to the beach because the weather was so beautiful. It took me about an hour to get ready. I found my bathing suit, towel, sunglasses and a good book. (**1.**) _____ .

Then I packed all these things in my beach bag. Finally, I was ready. (**2.**) _____ . I saw it was raining. I waited for it to stop, but it continued. Unfortunately, I had to stay home yesterday.

Activity 7	**Irregular Past Tense Verbs**

Answer the following questions. Use the irregular form of the simple past tense. Use verbs from the list in Grammar and Sentence Structure: Past Tense of Irregular Verbs on page 99. The first one has been done for you.

1. When were you born?

   I was born in 1977.

2. How did you feel yesterday?

3. Where did you go last weekend?

4. When did you see a movie?

5. What did you buy last week?

6. Whom did you speak with yesterday?

7. When did you leave for school this morning?

8. When did you do your homework?

GRAMMAR AND SENTENCE STRUCTURE:
Making *Be* Negative

When you want to make a sentence with *be* negative, you use the word *not*. *Not* comes after the form of *be*.

Paula was <u>not</u> home.   The CDs were <u>not</u> in their cases.

See Grammar and Sentence Structure: Simple Past Tense: Statements and Questions on pages 92–93 for a review of the forms of *be*.

Past Tense Verb Forms: Negatives

Verb *be*	I **was not**	we **were not**
	you **were not**	you (plural) **were not**
	he / she / it **was not**	they **were not**

NOTE: Some contractions are possible with the verb *be* in negative form.

was not = wasn't   were not = weren't

Careful! Be sure that the apostrophe (') is placed directly before the letter *t*. Remember that the apostrophe in negatives takes the place of the letter *o*.

Incorrect:	She is'nt my sister.
Incorrect:	She isn,t my sister.
Correct:	She isn't my sister. (*Or:* She's not my sister.)

Incorrect:	I was'nt in class yesterday.
Incorrect:	I wasn,t in class yesterday.
Correct:	I wasn't in class yesterday.

WRITER'S NOTE: Using Contractions

It is important to remember that contractions might be too informal for academic writing. Ask your instructor if using contractions in this course is acceptable.

| Activity 8 | Practicing Negative *Be* Verbs in the Past |

Read the following paragraph. Write the correct form of the be *verb in the blanks. Be sure to use the negative form where indicated. The first one has been done for you.*

Paragraph 46

Moving to the United States

My name is Panadda, and I (**1.**) __was__ born in Thailand. I (**2.** negative)_____

the first child. My sister Suntri (**3.**) _____ born three years before I

(**4.**) _____ born. My parents (**5.** negative) _____ rich, but they

(**6.**) _____ always happy. They (**7.**) _____ hard workers. In 1995,

we moved to the United States. Everyone in my family (**8.**) _____ very excited. We

(**9.**) _____ also scared. My parents (**10.** negative) _____ able to speak

English. When we arrived, they began English classes. My sister and I started school. We

(**11.** negative) _____ comfortable in the classroom because we didn't

know the language. After a few years, we learned the language and the culture of the

United States.

GRAMMAR AND SENTENCE STRUCTURE:
Other Negative Verbs

All other negative verbs in English are formed in the same way in the past tense. Just write *did not* and the simple verb. Look at these examples.

Verb *live* (negative past)	I **did not live**	we **did not live**
	you **did not live**	you (plural) **did not live**
	he / she / it **did not live**	they **did not live**

NOTE: Contraction: *did not* = *didn't*

Incorrect:	Ahmed no finish his homework.
Incorrect:	Ahmed no finished his homework.
Correct:	Ahmed did not (didn't) finish his homework.

Activity 9	Practicing Negative Verbs in the Past

Write the words as correct sentences with past tense negative verbs. The first one has been done for you.

1. Carmen / live (negative) / in Connecticut / in 1997.

   Carmen did not / didn't live in Connecticut in 1997.
   _____

2. Shelley / study (negative) / engineering.

   _____

3. Herbert's parents / visit (negative) / him last year.

   _____

4. Dinosaurs / have (negative) / large brains.

   _____

5. John / help (negative) / me with my homework!

   _____

NEGATIVE VERB REVIEW

In this unit, you learned about past tense verbs, questions, and negatives. This activity will help you review what you have learned.

Editing

Activity 10	Editing: Writing Negative Sentences with Contractions

WWW

**On the Web
Try Unit 4
Activity 6**

The sentences below are false. Work with a partner and rewrite each sentence, using the negative form of the verb to make the sentence true. Then write a correct sentence. Follow the example. Some verbs are regular and some are irregular. Refer to the complete list of irregular verbs in Appendix 5.

1. Winston Churchill was a leader of Mexico.

   Winston Churchill wasn't a leader of Mexico. He was a leader of Great Britain.

2. Confucius lived in Japan. _____

   _____

3. Pelé played basketball. _____

   _____

4. The Beatles sang in Arabic. _____

   _____

5. The *Titanic* sank in the Pacific Ocean. _____

   _____

6. The Statue of Liberty came from Italy. _____

   _____

7. Thomas Edison invented the radio. _____

   _____

8. Stephen King wrote *Romeo and Juliet*. _____

   _____

9. The prophet Mohammed spoke Hindi. _____

   _____

10. Marilyn Monroe was an engineer. _____

    _____

Activity 11   **Simple Past Tense Review**

Read the following paragraph. Change the verbs in parentheses to the past tense. Write the negative form where indicated. The first one has been done for you.

Paragraph 47

Bob's Horrible Day

Bob (**1.** have) ___had___ a horrible day on Monday. First, he (**2.** be) _____

supposed to get up at 6 A.M., but his alarm clock (**3.** work, negative) _____ . He

(**4.** wake up) _____ at 8 A.M. There (**5.** be) _____ no hot water for a

shower, so he had to use cold water. After that, his car (**6.** start, negative) _____ ,

and he had to take the bus. When Bob (**7.** get) _____ to work, his boss (**8.** yell)

_____ at him for being late. Next, his computer (**9.** crash) _____ ,

and he (**10.** lose) _____ all of his documents. He (**11.** stay) _____ at

work until midnight to redo the documents. Bob (**12.** decide) _____ to stay home

the next day because he (**13.** be) _____ too tired from all his bad luck.

COMPOUND SENTENCES WITH *BUT*

One common sentence connector is *but*. This word is often used to make compound sentences. The connector *but* shows a contrast.

Compound Sentences with *But*

The connector *but* indicates a contrast between the ideas it connects. Study this example.

Two Simple Sentences	One Compound Sentence
I bought a car. John bought a truck.	I bought a car, *but* John bought a truck.

WWW

**On the Web
Try Unit 4
Activity 7**

WWW

**On the Web
Try Unit 4
Activity 5**

SENTENCE DEVELOPMENT

This example is a compound sentence because it is two complete sentences connected by the word *but*. It has two separate subjects and two separate verbs.

I <u>bought</u> a car, but <u>John</u> <u>bought</u> a truck
SUBJ. VERB   SUBJ.   VERB

Look at another example.

Two Simple Sentences	One Compound Sentence
She studied for the exam. She didn't pass it.	She studied for the exam, *but* she didn't pass it.

NOTE: Notice the comma before *but*. You must put a comma before a connector in a compound sentence.

NOTE: Sometimes *but* is not a connector. In these cases, it is a preposition that means the same as the word *except*. Consider these examples:

<u>We</u> <u>visited</u> all of the countries in South America *but* Chile and Argentina.
SUBJ. VERB

<u>All</u> of the new cars but this one <u>are</u> luxury cars.
SUBJ.   VERB

These two sentences are simple sentences. There is only one subject-verb relationship in each sentence.

Activity 12	Compound Sentence Review

Read the following sentences. Some are compound sentences and some are simple. First, identify the type of sentence as S (simple) or C (compound). Then if the sentence is compound, insert a comma where it is necessary. The first three have been done for you.

1. ___S___ The girls practiced every day.

2. ___S___ They didn't win the tennis tournament.

3. ___C___ The girls practiced every day, but they didn't win the tennis tournament.

4. _____ The committee members made a decision but the manager didn't like it.

5. _____ Neal worked with his father at the shoe store for almost twenty years.

6. _____ We went to Canada but we didn't visit Toronto.

7. _____ With the recent increase in crime in that area of the city, the local residents there

    are worried about their safety.

8. _____ Summer is a good time to practice outdoor sports but winter is not.

9. _____ All of the workers but Marian arrived at yesterday's income tax meeting on time.

10. _____ Saudi Arabia and Kuwait import equipment, cars, food, and medicine.

11. _____ The chairs in the living room are made of pine but the chairs in my office are made

of oak.

12. _____ All of the chairs in the kitchen but this one are made of maple.

| Activity 13 | **Writing Compound Sentences** |

Read these charts. They give information about two brothers.

Name:	*Andrew Bright*
Born:	*January 14, 1915*
Died:	*March 23, 1985*
Home City:	*Washington, DC*
Education:	*High school*
Work:	*Firefighter*
Family:	*Wife and five children*
Hobbies:	*Singing*

Name:	*Ian Bright*
Born:	*May 1, 1920*
Died:	*September 12, 1992*
Home City:	*Chicago, Illinois*
Education:	*Bachelor's degree*
Work:	*High school math teacher*
Family:	*single*
Hobbies:	*Playing baseball*

Now read the incorrect statements below about the brothers. Then write a compound sentence with but. *Use the information in the charts. The first one has been done for you.*

1. They were born on the same day.

   Andrew was born on January 14, but Ian was born on May 1.

2. The brothers were born in the same year.

   _____

3. They both sang as a hobby.

   _____

4. Both brothers were married.

   _____

5. They lived in the same city.

   _____

6. They had the same level of education.

   _____

7. Both men had the same kind of job.

   _____

8. They died on the same date.

   _____

Activity 14 | Interviewing Your Classmates

Circulate around the classroom and ask different classmates the following questions. Write down the answers. When you have finished, complete the sentences using information about yourself and the information you received from your classmates. The first one has been done for you.

1. Where are you from? Classmate's Answer: Peru _____

   I am from Kuwait, but José is from Peru. _____

2. What did you eat last night for dinner? _____

   _____

3. Where was your last vacation? _____

   _____

4. Why did you come to this school? _____

_____

5. What country do you want to visit? _____

_____

Editing

| Activity 15 | **Editing: Grammar and Sentence Review** |

Read the following paragraph. Find and correct the 14 errors. If you need some help locating the errors, look at the numbers in parentheses on the left. This number tells you how many errors are in each line. The first one has been done for you.

Paragraph 48

Muhammad Ibn Batuta

                              was
(3)   Ibn Batuta a famous moroccan traveler. He live
                      ∧

        in Morocco in the fourteenth century. When he

(1)   was a man young, he made a religious trip to

(1)   Mecca. However, Ibn Batuta loves to see new

        places so much that he continued to travel. This

(2)   was no his original plan but he continued on his

(1)   journey. He had many adventures during her

(1)   travels and he met many interesting people. After

(1)   he returned home, he did not forgot about his

(1)   journey. He wrote a book about his travels. this

(1)   book now gives us a lot of information important

(1)   about life in the fourteenth century. Also gives us

        more information about this interesting and

(1)   important man

Word Build•ing (wûrd bĭl′dĭng) *n.*

| Activity 16 | Word Building |

Study the following word forms. In the sentences on the right, choose the best word and write it in the blank space. Be sure to use the correct form of the verb. (Note: The word in bold is the original word that appears in the unit.)

Noun	Verb	Adjective	Sentence Practice
pride	Ø	**proud**	1. She was very _____ when she graduated
			2. I have a lot of _____ in my children.
excell**ence**	excel	**excellent**	3. Damon _____ in swimming when he was younger.
			4. That was an _____ movie!
communication	**communicate**	communicat**ive**	5. We _____ for three hours by phone yesterday.
			6. Roberto was shy, but now he is more _____ .
continuation	**continue**	continu**ous**/continu**al**	7. The students _____ to study after the semester ended.
			8. The _____ traffic noise gave me a headache.
culture	Ø	cultur**al**	9. Do you know about Indian _____.
			10. Kim and Jo's _____ differences are small.

Noun endings: -ence
Adjective endings: -ous, -al, -ive

Building Better Sentences

Correct and varied sentence structure is essential to the quality of your writing. For further practice, go to Practice 4 on page 238 in Appendix 16.

Activity 17   **Original Writing Practice**

Reread the paragraph about Lao-Tzu on page 95 and your answers to Activity 3 on page 96. You will use this kind of information to write in the past tense about an important person.

Think of an important person. Then follow these steps for writing and use the checklist below. Put a check (✓) next to each step as you complete it. Remember to write in the past tense. You may want to review What Is a Paragraph? in Unit 2 on page 42.

Step 1 _____ In your first sentence, tell the name of the person and why that person was important.

Step 2 _____ In your next sentence, write where the person was born.

Step 3 _____ In the next sentence, tell about the person's job.

Step 4 _____ In the next three or four sentences, tell a short story about the person.

Step 5 _____ Try to use the word *but* in one of the sentences in Step 4. Remember to use a comma!

Step 6 _____ Use a *negative verb* in one of the sentences in Step 4.

Step 7 _____ In the next sentence, write why you chose this person.

Checklist

✔ 1. ❑ Make sure every sentence has a subject and a verb.

✔ 2. ❑ Make sure the verbs are the correct form of the past tense.

✔ 3. ❑ Make sure every sentence begins with a capital letter.

✔ 4. ❑ Make sure that all the proper nouns (names, cities, countries, etc.) are capitalized.

✔ 5. ❑ Make sure every sentence ends with the correct punctuation.

✔ 6. ❑ Create a title for your paragraph.

Activity 18   **Peer Editing**

Choose someone that you work well with. Exchange papers from Activity 17 with that student. Read your partner's paragraph. Use Peer Editing Sheet 4 on page 259 to help you talk about your partner's work.

Activity 19   **Journal Writing**

EXTRA WRITING

Here are ten ideas for journal writing. Choose one or more of them to write about. Follow your teacher's directions. (We recommend that you skip a line after each line that you write. This gives your teacher a place to write comments.)

1. Describe a pet you had in the past. What was the pet's name? What kind of animal was it? How long did you have this pet? Why did you like this pet? (*Or:* Why did you dislike this pet?)

2. Describe a home you lived in when you were a child. How big was the house? What color was the house? Where was the house? Did you like the house? What was your favorite room in the house?

3. Write about a movie you saw or a book you read. Did you like it? Who was your favorite character? What was the story about? Did the author have a message for the readers of this book?

4. Write about what you did last weekend. Where did you go? Who did you go with? Did you enjoy it?

5. Write about a person you used to know. Who was this person? Where did you meet this person? What was special about this person?

6. Write about an important event in your life. How old were you? What happened? Why is this event important to you?

7. Describe a holiday that you and your family spent together. What was the occasion? Which family members were there? What did you do?

8. Write about something embarrassing that happened to you. How old were you? What happened? Why were you embarrassed? Who saw this happen? How did you feel afterwards?

9. Write about a day you spent outdoors. What did you do? Where did you go? Who did you go with? What specific activities did you do? How was the weather?

10. Describe a vacation you took. Where did you go? What did you do? Who went on this vacation with you? How old were you when you went on this trip? Did you like this vacation?

> **MORE WRITING**

For extra writing practice, see the activities in Unit 8, Appendix 17, and the *Great Sentences* website: http://esl.college.hmco.com/students.

Describing Actions

GOAL: To learn how to write in the present progressive tense

GRAMMAR AND SENTENCE STRUCTURE: Present progressive tense; adverbs of manner

SENTENCE DEVELOPMENT: Compound sentences with *and*; compound sentences with *so*

USING THE PRESENT PROGRESSIVE

When good writers write about actions that are happening at the moment, they often use the present progressive tense.

GRAMMAR AND SENTENCE STRUCTURE: Present Progressive Tense for Current Actions

The present progressive tense (*be* + verb + *ing*) is often used to describe actions that are happening right now. Review the chart below before beginning the activities in this unit. (See Appendix 6 for spelling rules of verbs ending in *-ing*.)

Present Progressive Tense

I	**am eating**	we	**are eating**
you	**are eating**	you (plural)	**are eating**
he / she / it	**is eating**	they	**are eating**

114

I	**am walk*ing***	we	**are walk*ing***
you	**are walk*ing***	you (plural)	**are walk*ing***
he / she / it	**is walk*ing***	they	**are walk*ing***

Careful! Some verbs in English do *not* usually take the progressive tense because they are not action verbs. Here are some common stative, or non-action, verbs: *be, have, see, love, believe, own, want.* (See Appendix 7 for more information.)

Activity 1   **Identifying Present Progressive Tense**

Read the following paragraph about a Sunday afternoon at the zoo. Underline all the present progressive verbs. There are 16.

Paragraph 49

**On the Web
Try Unit 5
Activity 1**

A Day Trip for the Johnson Family

EXAMPLE PARAGRAPH

The Johnson family lives in Chicago. It is a large family with Mr. and Mrs. Johnson, their two sons Keith and Kevin, and their daughter Rosie. Today is a special day for the Johnsons. They are visiting the Brookfield Zoo. Mr. Johnson and Rosie love monkeys, so they are walking to the monkey **exhibit**. They are watching the chimpanzees and orangutans. The chimps are playing with each other, and some of them are swinging from ropes. The monkeys look like they are having a good time. One orangutan is looking at the **crowd** of people. The other orangutan is eating a banana. At the other end of the zoo, the rest of the Johnson family is walking to the lion exhibit. Keith and Kevin are talking about how powerful the male lion looks. This lion is walking around and **yawning**. Mrs. Johnson is talking to her sons. She is telling a story about a **safari** that she took when she was younger. Keith and Kevin are listening to their mother's story, and they are asking Mrs. Johnson to take them on a safari.

exhibit: display, performance

crowd: large group

yawning: opening its mouth to show sleepiness or hunger

safari: a trip in the jungle, often to see wild animals

| **Activity 2** | **Writing from Picture Prompts** |

Study the picture of Bruce and his friends. Then read the paragraph. Fill in the missing verbs and sentence based on what you see in the picture.

Paragraph 50

A University Student's Room

Tomorrow is a big day for Bruce. His mother is coming to visit him for the first time at college. Bruce is very excited, but he is also worried. His dorm room is a mess. This is why he called all his friends to come help him. His good friend Lina (**1.**) _____ the floor because the carpet is very dirty. Bruce's friend Joe (**2.**) _____ some of Bruce's clothes to the laundry. At the same time, Bruce's roommate Paul (**3.**) _____ all of the empty pizza boxes and soda cans. Bruce (**4.**) _____ _____ . Bruce feels very lucky to have such good friends, and he is sure that the room will be ready for his mother's visit.

| Activity 3 | **Writing from Picture Prompts** |

Study the picture of the soccer game. Read the prompts that are connected to each action.
Complete the sentences on the next page using the present progressive tense.

Other fans/wave/flags and banners

Some fans/cheer/for their team

The coach/watch/the ball

The referee/run/toward the goal

The forward/hope/the shot will be a goal.

The soccer ball/go/into the net

The goalkeeper/jump/for the ball

1. The soccer ball _____ .

2. The goalkeeper _____ .

3. The coach _____ .

4. The referee _____ .

5. The forward _____ .

6. Some fans _____ .

7. Other fans _____ .

When you complete the sentences, compare them to a classmate's sentences.

Activity 4   Writing a Paragraph

Rewrite the sentences in paragraph form. Try to use your imagination and add some extra information and adjectives about this game. Create a title for the paragraph.

_____

The soccer game between Juventus and Manchester United is very exciting. Many things are

happening right now!

_____

_____

_____

_____

_____

_____

_____

_____

USING THE CONNECTOR *AND*

In Unit 4, you practiced using the connector *but* to make compound sentences. In the following activities, you will practice another common connector—*and*.

Compound Sentences with *And*

Good writers often use the connector *and* to join words and ideas. Here are some common examples.

1. **And is used to join two (or more) words that are in the same grammar category (or group).**

   Example A: In the following sentence, *and* joins two <u>nouns</u> and makes the subject of the sentence plural.

   > Bobby *and* Jenny go to Oak Ridge Elementary School.

   This sentence means:

   > Bobby goes to Oak Ridge Elementary School.

   > Jenny goes to Oak Ridge Elementary School.

   Example B: In the following sentence, *and* joins two <u>nouns</u> and makes the object of the sentence plural.

   > My sister loves pizza *and* spaghetti.

   This sentence means:

   > My sister loves pizza.

   > My sister loves spaghetti.

   Example C: In the following sentence, *and* joins two <u>verbs</u> in a sentence.

   > Ricardo works *and* studies at the university.

   This sentence means:

   > Ricardo works at the university.

   > Ricardo studies at the university.

   Example D: In the following sentence, *and* joins two <u>adjectives</u> in a sentence.

   > The weather was hot *and* muggy.

   This sentence means:

   > The weather was hot.

   > The weather was muggy.

2. **The connector *and* is also used to form compound sentences.** Remember from Unit 3 that a compound sentence is two sentences joined by a comma and a connecting word. A compound sentence has two subjects and two verbs.

SENTENCE DEVELOPMENT

Example A:

Irene works at the mall, *and* her brother visits her store every day.

This sentence means:

Irene works at the mall.

Irene's brother visits her store every day.

NOTE: When you join these two sentences, you do not need to repeat *Irene* after the connector. You can use the possessive adjective *her*.

Example B:

Joanna is washing the car, *and* her mother is cooking dinner.

This sentence means:

Joanna is washing the car.

Joanna's mother is cooking dinner.

| Activity 5 | Compound Sentence Practice |

**On the Web
Try Unit 5
Activity 2**

Connect the two simple sentences into a compound sentence by using the connector and. *Remember to put a comma (,) before* and. *The first one has been done for you.*

1. John is watching a movie. Ann is eating popcorn.

   John is watching a movie, and Ann is eating popcorn.

2. Oranges contain a lot of vitamin C. Milk has a large amount of vitamin D.

   _____

3. Bolivia is a landlocked country in South America. Switzerland is a landlocked country in Europe.

   _____

4. Those pants are the perfect color for you. They are on sale.

   _____

5. I am planting marigold seeds. I hope they will grow quickly.

   _____

| Activity 6 | **Analyzing Compound Sentences with *And*** |

Read the paragraph and complete the sentence analysis that follows.

Paragraph 51

Jobs for the Future

Dharma and Greta are studying engineering at the University of Georgia. Dharma lives in a dormitory, and Greta is her roommate. They are going to graduate at the end of the year. Both Dharma and Greta want to get good jobs in the private sector when they graduate. Dharma hopes to work for Motorola, and Greta wants to get a job with the Georgia Power Company.

Now read each sentence below. Rewrite the information using two sentences instead of one. The first one has been done for you.

1. Dharma and Greta are studying engineering at the University of Georgia.

    Meaning: _Dharma is studying engineering at the University of Georgia._

    Greta is studying engineering at the University of Georgia.

2. Dharma lives in a dormitory, and Greta is her roommate.

    Meaning: _____

    _____

3. Dharma and Greta are going to graduate at the end of the year.

    Meaning: _____

    _____

4. Both Dharma and Greta want to get good jobs in the private sector when they graduate.

    Meaning: _____

    _____

5. Dharma hopes to work for Motorola, and Greta wants to get a job with the Georgia Power Company.

    Meaning: _____

    _____

USING THE CONNECTOR *SO*

So is another connector that good writers use in compound sentences. This connector shows a cause and a result.

Compound Sentences with *So*

The connector *so* shows a result. The first subject and verb gives the "cause" and the second subject and verb gives the "result."

CAUSE   RESULT
I was hungry, <u>so</u> I ate a sandwich.

                CAUSE   RESULT
Leslie has a big exam tomorrow, <u>so</u> she is studying at the library.

            CAUSE   RESULT
The children had a long day, <u>so</u> they are taking a nap now.

NOTE: Another word for a subject and verb is **clause**. In each example there are two clauses. These sentences are compound. Remember to use a comma before *so* when it shows cause and result.

| Activity 7 | **Combining Sentences with *So*** |

Read the two sentences. Write C (for cause) or R (for result) on the line to show what kind of sentence each is. Then combine them into a compound sentence. Put the cause first, then the connector so, *and then the result. Be sure to put a comma before* so *and add a period at the end of the sentence. The first one has been done for you.*

(Note: Sometimes you will need to change nouns to pronouns—for example, the boy ➔ *him or the car* ➔ *it.)*

On the Web
Try Unit 5
Activity 3
Activity 7

1a. ___C___ I was thirsty.

 b. ___R___ I drank three glasses of water.

    I was thirsty, so I drank three glasses of water. _____

2a. _____ We didn't play tennis.

 b. _____ It rained really hard.

    _____

3a. _____ We took the cat to the vet.

b. _____ The cat was very sick.

_____

4a. _____ The audience loved the show.

b. _____ They applauded wildly.

_____

5a. _____ Jonathan didn't feel well.

b. _____ Jonathan didn't go to the party.

_____

6a. _____ I didn't buy the record.

b. _____ The record was very expensive.

_____

7a. _____ The plane didn't leave on time.

b. _____ We arrived at our destination late.

_____

8a. _____ She forgot to set her alarm clock.

b. _____ She woke up late.

_____

Activity 8 | **Scenarios: Writing Compound Sentences with *So* and the Present Progressive**

Study the following pictures. Write what you think is happening based on what you see. Be sure to use the connector so *and the present progressive in your compound sentences. The first one has been done for you.*

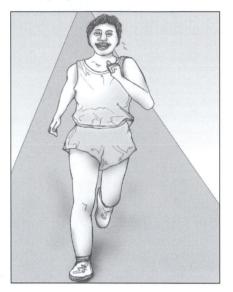

1. The woman wants to lose weight,

   so she is exercising.

   _____

   _____

2. _____

   _____

   _____

3. _____

   _____

4. _____

_____

_____

_____

_____

_____

5. _____

_____

_____

_____

_____

_____

6. _____

_____

_____

_____

_____

_____

| Activity 9 | **Compound Sentence Review** |

Read the following sentences. Some of the sentences are compound sentences and some are simple. First, identify the type of sentence as S (simple) or C (compound). Then, if the sentence is compound, insert a comma where necessary. The first two have been done for you.

WWW
On the Web
Try Unit 5
Activity 4
Activity 6

1. __S__ My brother and I went hiking and fishing last weekend.

2. __C__ The motorcycle is in the garage, and the car is in the driveway.

3. _____ Harry and Darlene went to the picnic yesterday and the party last night.

4. _____ I don't know the answer to the question so I will ask the teacher.

5. _____ How many times have you visited Europe and Asia?

6. _____ There are many great places to visit in this city so you can't see them all in one day.

7. _____ The main agricultural product from the countries in that area of Central Asia is cotton.

8. _____ A noun is a word like *cat*, and a verb is an action word such as *eat*.

9. _____ Lisana works for IBM but she doesn't have a computer engineering degree.

10. _____ Where did you get those beautiful earrings and bracelets?

11. _____ The capital of Sudan is Khartoum and it is the most populated city in the country.

12. _____ The traffic was terrible so Lance missed his plane.

WRITER'S NOTE: Use Sentence Variety

Many students who are studying English write short sentences. These sentences usually follow the same pattern: simple subject + simple verb. Good writers do not repeat the same sentence patterns too often. They write some short sentences and some longer sentences. Vary your writing with both simple and compound sentences. Use connectors to show that you can write more advanced sentences in English.

ADVERBS

Adverbs are another interesting word group in English. There are several kinds of adverbs in English. Most of them describe verbs.

GRAMMAR AND SENTENCE STRUCTURE:
Common Adverbs of Manner

In Unit 2 you studied adjectives. These are words that describe nouns.

Did you see the <u>beautiful</u> baby? The baby is <u>beautiful</u>.

In these sentences, the adjective *beautiful* describes the baby.

Adverbs also describe, but adverbs usually describe verbs.

Kerry picked up the puppy <u>carefully</u>.

My sister studies <u>hard</u>.

In these examples, the adverbs describe how the action is done. *How* shows manner.

How did Kerry pick up the puppy? <u>Carefully</u>.

How does my sister study? <u>Hard</u>.

NOTE: Adverbs of manner usually end in *-ly* and usually follow the verb.

Here is a list of some common adverbs of manner that describe actions:

quickly   easily   nervously   carefully   happily   slowly

suddenly   silently   correctly   fast*   hard*   well*

* These adverbs do *not* use the *-ly* form.

Activity 10   **Practice with Adverbs**

Read each sentence. In the blank, write an adverb that describes the action of the verb (underlined).
You may choose from the list of common adverbs of manner or use your own adverbs.

1. Joann <u>is studying</u> _____ in the library.

2. She <u>jumped</u> on the bus _____ because it was raining.

3. Mary Ann <u>spoke</u> _____ at the conference.

4. David <u>is doing</u> _____ in this class. He never studies!

5. Norma <u>cried</u> _____ during the movie.

6. Leslie <u>typed</u> the letter _____. I thought she would never finish.

7. Nathalie <u>read</u> the directions _____. She did not want to make

a mistake.

8. I have a cold, so I do not <u>feel</u> _____ today.

9. Maria and Faisal <u>passed</u> the test _____ because they studied very

_____ for it.

10. Lawrence <u>opened</u> the door _____ because he was afraid.

| Activity 11 | **Writing What You See: Describing Actions** |

Write a paragraph based on observation. Choose a place from which to observe people, for example, a park, a mall, or a cafeteria. You may also use a show on television or an illustration in a magazine. Be sure to choose something that has several people who are doing different actions. Use the following questions to help you write a paragraph. The paragraph has been started for you.

- Look at the people. What are they doing?
- Write about an object. What is happening with it?
- Remember to use the connectors *and* and *so* if possible.

There is a lot of action happening right now. _____

_____

_____

_____

_____

_____

_____

_____

_____

_____

_____

_____

_____

_____

_____

Editing

Activity 12   **Editing: Grammar and Sentence Review**

Read the following paragraph. There are ten mistakes in the paragraph: two (2) mistakes with compound sentences, two (2) mistakes with adverbs, two (2) mistakes with verbs, two (2) mistakes with adjectives, and two (2) mistakes with capitalization. Find and correct the errors. The first one has been done for you.

Paragraph 52

The Squirrel

              is

A small brown squirrel climbing a tree. He looks like a
                ∧

young squirrel. His tail is twitching nervously and his nose is

moving quick. I think he is looking for food. Now the squirrel

brown is on a long tree branch. He wants to jump to another

tree. The squirrel hears something so he looks down. he is

coming down from the tree tall. Someone dropped a few

pieces of chocolate chip cookie. These pieces lying on the

grass. the squirrel is walking toward the food, and he is

inspecting it. He is putting it in his mouth. His tail is moving

rapid. The little brown squirrel is now eating happily.

Word Build•ing (wûrd bĭl'dĭng) n.

Activity 13   **Word Building**

Study the following word forms. In the sentences on the right, choose the best word and write it in the blank space. Be sure to use the right form of the verb. (Note: The word in bold is the original word that appears in the unit.)

Noun	Verb	Adjective	Sentence Practice
beauty	Ø	**beautiful**	1. Did you see the _____ sunset yesterday?
			2. That painting is a thing of _____.
luck	Ø	**lucky**	3. The _____ lottery winner won $5 million.
			4. It was bad _____ that our team lost the game.
thirst	Ø	**thirsty**	5. If you are _____, drink some iced tea.
			6. Keith is playing tennis. He is probably suffering from _____.
fishing	fish	Ø	7. _____ is a relaxing sport.
			8. We _____ in the lake behind our house.
hiking	hike	Ø	9. Kat _____ every weekend.
			10. Do you like _____?

Noun endings: -ing
Adjective endings: -ful, -y

Building Better Sentences

Correct and varied sentence structure is essential to the quality of your writing. For further practice, go to Practice 5 on page 239 in Appendix 16.

Activity 14   **Original Writing Practice**

Imagine that you are a TV news reporter. Right now you are at the location of some problem. Describe what is happening around you. Use your imagination!

Now follow these steps for writing and use the checklist below. Put a check (✓) next to each step as you complete it. You may want to review What Is a Paragraph? in Unit 2 on page 42.

Step 1 _____ In your first sentence, tell where you are and what you are watching.

Step 2 _____ In your next sentence, describe the person, people, or things you see. Use adjectives to give a clear idea to your reader.

Step 3 _____ In the next two to four sentences, describe what the people are doing.

Step 4 _____ Use one or two adverbs in the sentences in Step 3. Remember to place them correctly (usually after the verb).

Step 5 _____ Use *and* or *so* in one of the sentences. Remember to use a comma to separate the two clauses.

Step 6 _____ In the next sentence, write what you think the people are thinking at this moment.

Step 7 _____ In the final sentence, write your opinion about these people.

Checklist

✔1. ❑ Make sure every sentence has a subject and a verb.

✔2. ❑ Be sure that the compound sentences have two subjects and verbs (clauses).

✔3. ❑ Make sure you use the present progressive verbs correctly.

✔4. ❑ Make sure every sentence begins with a capital letter.

✔5. ❑ Make sure every sentence ends with the correct punctuation.

✔6. ❑ Create a title for your paragraph.

Activity 15   Peer Editing

Choose someone that you work well with. Exchange papers from Activity 14 with that student. Read your partner's paragraph. Use Peer Editing Sheet 5 on page 261 to help you talk about your partner's work.

Activity 16   Journal Writing

EXTRA WRITING

Here are ten ideas for journal writing. Choose one or more of them to write about. Follow your teacher's directions. (We recommend that you skip a line after each line that you write. This gives your teacher a place to write comments.)

1. Watch several minutes of a television program. Describe what is happening in the show.

2. Describe how your life is now. Include your studies, your living arrangements, and your free time.

3. Imagine that you are a private investigator. Imagine a specific character or person. Write down everything that person did for five minutes.

4. Find a picture in a magazine. Choose a picture of many people who are doing different things. Write a paragraph that describes what each person is doing.

5. Imagine that you are visiting the zoo. What are the animals doing? Write a paragraph that tells what at least five different kinds of animals are doing. Use the connectors *and*, *but*, or *so* to combine short sentences into longer sentences.

6. Imagine that you are in a large city like Chicago, Illinois, or Toronto, Canada. Walk around the city and write down the things that you see. What is happening in this large city?

7. Imagine that you are walking down the street, and you see your favorite movie star walk into a café. Follow this person. What is he/she doing?

8. Write a letter to your friend explaining what you are doing in this class. Tell about the assignments that you have and the writing skills that you are practicing.

9. If you have a pet, watch it closely for ten minutes. What is it doing? Where is it going? Is it playing? Jumping? Making noise?

10. Imagine that you are a news reporter for a movie magazine. You are at the Academy Awards presentation. What are the people doing? Name some of the famous actors. (This word means male and female actors.) What are they doing? What are they wearing? What are they saying to their friends? What are they wondering?

MORE WRITING

For extra writing practice, see the activities in Unit 8, Appendix 17, and the *Great Sentences* website: http://esl.college.hmco.com/students.

Writing About the Future

GOAL: To learn how to write in the future tense

GRAMMAR AND SENTENCE STRUCTURE: *Be going to* and *will* for future: statements, questions, negatives; time words to show the future; articles; using commas in a list

SENTENCE DEVELOPMENT: Complex sentences; answering questions with *because*

TALKING ABOUT THE FUTURE

There are many ways to talk about events that will happen in the future. One way is to use *be going to*. You can use *be going to* when you talk about future plans or when you want to make predictions—or guesses—about the future.

GRAMMAR AND SENTENCE STRUCTURE: *Be Going To*: Statements and Questions

It is easy to make a sentence with *be going to*. Just put *be* + *going to* in front of the base form of the verb.

Be Going To: Statements

Verb *study*

I	**am going to study**	we	**are going to study**
you	**are going to study**	you (plural)	**are going to study**
he / she / it	**is going to study**	they	**are going to study**

Study these examples.

Incorrect: We going to go to the store in a few minutes.

Correct: We are going to go to the store in a few minutes.

Incorrect: I am going to a sandwich for lunch.

Correct: I am going to buy a sandwich for lunch.

Incorrect: According to the radio report, the weather going to be severe tonight.

Correct: According to the radio report, the weather is going to be severe tonight.

Be Going To: Questions

Verb *fly*

Am I going to fly . . . ?	**Are we going to fly** . . . ?
Are you going to fly . . . ?	**Are you** (plural) **going to fly** . . . ?
Is he / she / it going to fly . . . ?	**Are they going to fly** . . . ?

On the Web
Try Unit 6
Activity 1
Activity 5

Study these examples.

Incorrect: Jim and Dave are going to buy a new car?

Correct: Are Jim and Dave going to buy a new car?

Incorrect: They going to see a movie this afternoon?

Correct: Are they going to see a movie this afternoon?

Incorrect: Did you going to visit your parents in December?

Correct: Are you going to visit your parents in December?

Activity 1   Making Predictions

Look at each picture. Make a prediction about what will happen. Use the correct form of be going to. *Write complete sentences.*

1. _____   2. _____

   _____   _____

   _____   _____

   _____   _____

3. _____

   _____

4. _____

_____

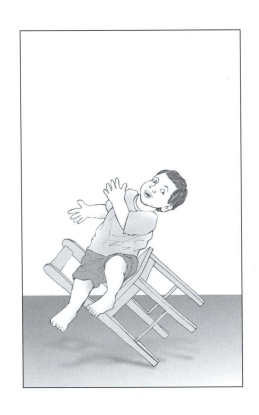

5. _____   6. _____

_____   _____

_____   _____

_____   _____

WRITER'S NOTE: Don't Use *Gonna* in Writing

Speakers of English often pronounce *going to* as *gonna* in informal speech. However, do not use *gonna* in writing. You must write out the words completely.

| *Incorrect writing:* | I'm gonna buy a new shirt. |
| *Correct writing:* | I'm going to buy a new shirt. |

GRAMMAR AND SENTENCE STRUCTURE:
Will: Statements and Questions

Will can also be used to talk about future plans. It's easy to use *will* in a sentence about future plans. Just put *will* in front of the base form of the verb.

Will: Statements

Verb *buy*

I	**will** buy	we	**will** buy
you	**will** buy	you (plural)	**will** buy
he / she / it	**will** buy	they	**will** buy

Study these examples.

Incorrect:	She will goes to school tomorrow.
Correct:	She will go to school tomorrow.
Incorrect:	They will are watch a new movie tonight.
Correct:	They will watch a new movie tonight.
Incorrect:	We will talking to the teacher next week.
Correct:	We will talk to the teacher next week.

Will: Questions

Verb *make*

Will I **make** . . . ?	**Will** we **make** . . . ?
Will you **make** . . . ?	**Will** you (plural) **make** . . . ?
Will he / she / it **make** . . . ?	**Will** they **make** . . . ?

Study these examples.

Incorrect:	Rhonda will arrive soon?
Correct:	Will Rhonda arrive soon?
Incorrect:	Will Keith and Jason plays soccer this weekend?
Correct:	Will Keith and Jason play soccer this weekend?
Incorrect:	The students take their finals on time this semester?
Correct:	Will the students take their finals on time this semester?

Activity 2 — Writing About Future Plans

Look at Michael's schedule for next week. Answer the questions using complete sentences. The first one has been done for you. Notice both will *and* be going to *are used.*

Sunday	**Monday**	**Tuesday**	**Wednesday**	**Thursday**	**Friday**	**Saturday**
Meet Mom & Dad for lunch	Meeting with Mr. Green	Take dog to the veterinarian	Business report due to Ms. Simms	Buy groceries	Dinner with Andrea	Soccer game 6 pm

1. What is Michael going to do on Sunday?

   Michael is going to meet his mom and dad for lunch on Sunday.

2. Who will Michael meet on Monday?

   _____

3. When is he going to have dinner with Andrea?

   _____

4. Where is he going to take his pet?

   _____

5. What will he do on Thursday?

   _____

6. When is he going to play soccer?

   _____

7. What will he give to Ms. Simms on Wednesday?

   _____

Activity 3 | **Practicing with Paragraphs**

Review the sentences you wrote about Michael's schedule in Activity 2. Put them in correct time order, starting with Sunday. Write the sentences in paragraph form below. The beginning and the end of the paragraph have been done for you.

Michael's Busy Schedule

Michael is going to be a very busy man next week! First, he is going to meet his mom and dad for

lunch on Sunday.

_____

_____

_____

_____

_____

_____

_____

_____

_____

_____

_____

Finally, he is going to play soccer at six o'clock on Saturday. Michael is the busiest man I know!

USING TIME WORDS

Good writers include *time words* and *time phrases* in their writing. Time words and phrases give important information about *when* something happens.

GRAMMAR AND SENTENCE STRUCTURE:
Time Words and Phrases

Study this list of time words and phrases. Do you know the meanings of all of them?

first	tomorrow	in a minute	next week
next	next Saturday	later	next year
finally	next January	then	next time
after that	before that		

Time words usually occur at the beginning or the end of a sentence. However, they can sometimes occur in the middle of a sentence. Look at these examples of time words and phrases at the beginning and at the end of sentences.

We are going to go to the movies <u>on Saturday</u>.

<u>On Saturday</u>, we are going to go to the movies.

Angela is going to study in France <u>next year</u>.

<u>Next year</u>, Angela is going to study in France.

The airline will produce a new kind of jet <u>in the next few months</u>.

<u>In the next few months</u>, the airline will produce a new kind of jet.

We are going to paint the kitchen <u>first</u>.

<u>First</u>, we are going to paint the kitchen.

Notice that a comma immediately follows the time words and phrases at the beginning of the sentence.

On the Web
Try Unit 6
Activity 3
Activity 4

Activity 4   **Practicing with Time Words**

Fill in the blanks with these time words: then, next, first, after, Sunday, finally. One word can be used twice.

Paragraph 53

A Reunion to Remember

This year, our family reunion will be special because we are going to celebrate my Aunt

Laura's ninety-eighth birthday. (**1.**) _____ , everyone in our family will travel to

my aunt's town for the weekend. The (**2.**) _____ night, we are going to meet at

Aunt Laura's house and eat a big dinner. (**3.**) _____ dinner, we are going to bring

out a big birthday cake. (**4.**) _____ we will sing to her and give her presents. She

is going to love it! The (**5.**) _____ day, the whole family will meet in the city park for a big picnic. There will be food, games, and music for everyone. Aunt Laura will give a nice

speech to the family, too. On (**6.**) _____ , everyone will go to church with Aunt

Laura. (**7.**) _____ , our special celebration will be over, and everyone will return

home dreaming about next year's reunion.

| Activity 5 | **Responding to a Reading Passage** |

Read the paragraph and underline the ten future tense verbs. (Hint: Two of them might be difficult to find.) Then answer the questions that follow.

Paragraph 54

Carmen's Fifteenth Birthday

EXAMPLE PARAGRAPH

Next week Carmen Viera is going to be 15 years old, and her family has plans for a

special celebration for her. On her birthday, Carmen is going to wear a beautiful white

gown. First, she is going to go to church with her family and friends. After church is

over, they will go to a beautiful **ballroom**. Then they are going to have a party called a

quince. When Carmen arrives, she will perform some formal dances with her friends.

After that, everyone is going to dance, eat, and celebrate. Carmen can **hardly** wait. She

will never forget such a special day.

gown: a long, formal dress
ballroom: a large room where formal parties are held

quince: the Spanish word for fifteen; a traditional Latin birthday party that celebrates when a girl becomes a woman

hardly: with difficulty

1. How old is Carmen going to be next week?

_____

2. What is Carmen going to wear on her birthday?

_____

3. What is the first thing she is going to do on her birthday?

_____

4. Where is her *quince* party going to be held?

_____

5. What are Carmen and her friends going to do at the party?

_____

BE GOING TO AND WILL WITH NEGATIVES

You know how to use *be* + *going to* and *will* to talk about events that happen in the future. You learned how to make affirmative statements and how to ask questions about the future. It is also important to know how to talk about things that are not going to happen in the future.

GRAMMAR AND SENTENCE STRUCTURE:
Be Going To and *Will*: Negative

To make *be going to* negative, write the word *not* between the *be* verb and *going*. Study this chart of *be going to* with the negative *not*.

I	**am <u>not</u> going to study**	we	**are <u>not</u> going to study**
you	**are <u>not</u> going to study**	you (plural)	**are <u>not</u> going to study**
he / she / it	**is <u>not</u> going to study**	they	**are <u>not</u> going to study**

NOTE: You can make contractions with these negative verbs.

are not = aren't   is not = isn't

Study these examples.

Incorrect: I am going to not talk.

Correct: I am (I'm) not going to talk.

Incorrect: Jane not going to sing on Sunday.

Correct: Jane is not (isn't) going to sing on Sunday.

Incorrect: Brett and Erica no going to play soccer.

Correct: Brett and Erica are not (aren't) going to play soccer.

To make *will* negative, write the word *not* after it. Study this chart of *will* with the negative *not*.

I	**will not write**	we	**will not write**
you	**will not write**	you (plural)	**will not write**
he / she / it	**will not write**	they	**will not write**

NOTE: You can make contractions with these negative verbs.

will not = won't

Study these examples:

Incorrect:	They will not to come to the party.
Correct:	They will not (won't) come to the party.
Incorrect:	The president not make a speech on television tonight.
Correct:	The president will not (won't) make a speech on television tonight.
Incorrect:	My company will don't give me a raise this year.
Correct:	My company will not (won't) give me a raise this year.

Activity 6 **Writing Original Sentences**

Think of something important or special that you are going to do in the future. Answer these questions.

1. What is one important thing that you are going to do in your life?

   _____

   _____

2. How long will it take to do it?

   _____

3. What are you are going to do to accomplish this thing? (Write at least three things.)

   _____

   _____

   _____

   _____

4. How will you feel when you accomplish this thing? Why?

   _____

   _____

COMPLEX SENTENCES

In Unit 5, you learned that sentence variety is important. Good writers write both simple and compound sentences. There is another way to add variety to your sentence writing. You can put two clauses (each with a subject and verb) together when one of them begins with a different kind of connecting word.

Sentence Variety: Complex Sentences

One way to combine two sentences into one is to use a connecting word that is part of the sentence. Some of these connecting words are *after, before, because, if, although, since,* and *when.* Unlike the connectors in compound sentences (*and, but, so*), the connecting words in complex sentences are a necessary part of one of the sentences (clauses). This type of sentence is called a complex sentence. Look at these examples:

Compound sentence: Joe played tennis, and Vicky watched TV.

This sentence has three parts: sentence + the connector *and* + sentence.

> Joe played tennis / and / Vicky watched TV.

Complex sentence: Joe played tennis after Vicky watched TV.

This sentence has two parts: one simple sentence + one sentence that begins with the connecting word *after.*

> Joe played tennis / after Vicky watched TV.

The word *after* is not a part by itself. This word is part of the idea of *when* Vicky watched TV. The group of words with the connecting word must always be connected to another sentence. Otherwise, it is a *fragment.* (See Unit 1, page 17, for information on fragments.)

Here are a few more examples of complex sentences.

My mom is going to make dinner <u>when</u> my dad gets home.

Alana is going to get a full-time job <u>after</u> she graduates.

<u>As soon as</u> we get paid, we are going to buy some new clothes.

<u>Because</u> it is cold outside, they are going to wear jackets.

Commas in Complex Sentences

When a complex sentence begins with a clause that contains a connecting word, put a comma at the end of the clause.

                      CONNECTING WORD CLAUSE

Comma: <u>After she ate dinner</u>, she called up her friend.

                                    CONNECTING WORD CLAUSE

No comma: She called up her friend <u>after she ate dinner</u>.

*For more information on complex sentences, read about subordinating clauses in Appendix 13, page 229.

SENTENCE DEVELOPMENT

WRITER'S NOTE: Verbs in Complex Sentences

Here is a rule for writing complex sentences about the *future*: Use the *present tense* in the clause with the time word. Use the *future tense* in the other clause. Do not use future tense in both clauses.

Example:

When the rain stops, I'm going to rake the leaves.

| Activity 7 | **Identifying Sentence Types** |

On the Web
Try Unit 6
Activity 6

Read the following sentences. Some of the sentences are simple, some are compound, and some are complex. First, identify the type of sentence as S (simple), CD (compound), or CX (complex). If the sentence is compound or complex, insert a comma if necessary. The first three have been done for you.

1. ___S___ I'm going to go scuba diving next weekend.

2. ___CD___ My father is going to retire next year, but my mother is going to continue working.

3. ___CX___ After he came home from the beach, Gerardo took a shower.

4. _____ Irene is going to call you when she gets home from work.

5. _____ We're going to go to the mall and the beach next Sunday.

6. _____ Ariel is going to go to college next year but her brother is going to get a job.

7. _____ When the game is over we're going to Harvey's Grill.

8. _____ How often do you work out at the gym?

9. _____ Leslie and Serena are sisters but they don't get along very well.

10. _____ Billy and his friends went to the hockey game and cheered for their team.

11. _____ If the pilot gets sick during a flight the copilot takes over.

12. _____ The copilot plays an important role in the success of a flight.

| Activity 8 | **Writing Complex Sentences in the Future** |

Answer the following questions. Use time words in your answer. If the question includes a time word, write a complex sentence for your answer. You can use the connecting words in the Sentence Variety section on page 144. The first one has been done for you.

1. What are you going to do after you graduate?

   After I graduate, I am going to look for a job.

2. What are you going to do as soon as you finish this exercise?

   _____

3. What are you not going to do before you go to bed tonight?

   _____

4. When are you going to do your homework?

   _____

5. When are you going to eat dinner?

   _____

6. What are you going to do after you eat dinner?

   _____

ARTICLES *A*, *AN*, *THE*

A, *an*, and *the* are three of the shortest words in English, but they are also three of the most important words. These words are articles. They are very important in correct writing and speaking. In this section, you are going to learn about the uses of these three words.

GRAMMAR AND SENTENCE STRUCTURE:
Using Articles in a Sentence

Good writers always use articles in the correct places. There are many rules for using articles in English.

A/An—Indefinite Articles

Use *a/an* when you have a singular count noun and are talking about something in general. Use *a* if the next word begins with a consonant sound. Use *an* if the next word begins with a vowel sound.

> I bought <u>a</u> sweater.

> Wendy wants <u>an</u> ice cream cone.

There are some exceptions to the consonant/vowel rule. If the beginning letter *h* is silent (as in *honor*), use *an* before it. If the beginning letter *u* sounds like the word *you* (as in *university*), use *a* before it. Remember to pay attention to the *sound* of the beginning of the word, not the letter that it begins with.

Incorrect:	Meet me at the library in a hour.
Correct:	Meet me at the library in an hour.
Incorrect:	John bought an unique gift for his mother.
Correct:	John bought a unique gift for his mother.
Incorrect:	Does your last name begin with a *e* or a *n*?
Correct:	Does your last name begin with an *e* or an *n*?

The—Definite Article

The can be used with both singular and plural count and noncount* nouns. Here are some basic rules for using *the*.

1. Use *the* for the second (and subsequent) time you talk about something.

> I bought a sweater and a coat yesterday.

> *The* sweater is made of wool, but *the* coat is made of leather.

2. Use *the* when the speaker and the listener both know about or are familiar with the subject.

> Are you going to <u>the bank</u> this afternoon?

* Noncount nouns are nouns that do not use a plural form: money   butter   homework   gold   honesty

Examples: Honesty is important. (not *the honesty*)
           When people discuss politics, they often disagree. (not *the politics*)

(See Appendix 9 on page 223 for a short list of common noncount nouns.)

3. Use *the* when the noun you are referring to is unique—there is only one.

> The sun and the Earth are both in the Milky Way galaxy.

> The Eiffel Tower is a beautiful monument.

(See Appendix 8 on page 221 for a more complete list of when to use the article *the*.)

Article Use Chart

Study this chart to help you remember the basic rules for using articles:

When Your Meaning Is:	Singular Count Nouns*	Plural Count Nouns	Noncount Nouns
General	a	ø**	ø
General	an	ø	ø
Specific	the	the	the

*Count nouns are nouns that have a plural form:

cat—cats   woman—women   child—children   house—houses

**ø means do not use an article.

WRITER'S NOTE: Singular Count Nouns and Modifiers

A singular count noun (*car, woman*) can never stand on its own in a sentence. An article (*a, an, the*), a possessive adjective (*my, your, his*), or a quantifier (*one, another, some*) *must* come before it. (See Appendix 10 for more examples of possessive adjectives. See Appendix 11 for more examples of quantifiers.) Look at the following sentences.

Incorrect:	April owns dog.
Correct:	April owns a dog.
Incorrect:	I am reading book.
Correct:	I am reading my book.
Incorrect:	Give me spoon. This one is dirty.
Correct:	Give me another spoon. This one is dirty. (quantifier)

**On the Web
Try Unit 6
Activity 7**

Activity 9   **Articles**

Read the paragraph. Write a, an, *or* the *in the blanks.*

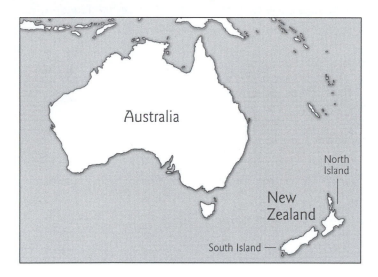

Paragraph 55

A World Traveler

Robert likes to travel a lot, and next year he is going to go on (**1.**) _____ excellent trip.

(**2.**) _____ trip is going to be to Egypt and New Zealand. He wants to meet a lot of new

people and try interesting food. While he is in Egypt, he is going to see (**3.**) _____ Great

Pyramids at Giza and (**4.**) _____ Sphinx of Cheops. He wants to take (**5.**) _____ cruise

down (**6.**) _____ Nile River, but it is probably going to be too expensive. After he visits

Egypt, he will fly to New Zealand to visit (**7.**) _____ cousin who lives there. His cousin's

name is Thomas. Robert and Thomas are going to hike along the coast of New Zealand for a

few weeks. They want to see (**8.**) _____ tuatara. Tuataras are lizards from (**9.**) _____

ancient reptile family. Because tuataras are **nocturnal**, it is going to be difficult to see them.

Finally, they will take (**10.**) _____ bike trip on (**11.**) _____ North Island. It is going to be

a fun trip.

nocturnal: active at night

| Activity 10 | Sentence Writing: Review |

Create complete sentences and questions from the prompts below. Remember to add the correct article (a, an, the) to the sentences where necessary. Use the correct verb tense, punctuation, and capitalization. The first one has been done for you.

1. robert / go (negative) / to / beach / tomorrow

   Robert is not going to go to the beach tomorrow.

2. laura's parents / visit / eiffel tower / in paris / last year

   _____

3. we / have / grammar test / next week (question)

   _____

4. weather / be / very / nice / for / picnic / last saturday

   _____

5. carol / bob / see / owl / in / tree / in their back yard / last night

   _____

6. you / go / movies / every friday night (question)

   _____

7. computer / not work / anymore

   _____

8. I / bring / apple / sandwich / for lunch yesterday

   _____

9. after nicholas / graduate last week / his sister / give him / expensive gift

   _____

10. my dad / buy / me / bike / for / my last birthday / but / I / want / puppy

   _____

QUESTIONS AND ANSWERS: STRUCTURES WITH *BECAUSE*

You have learned that one way to write complex sentences is with words such as *after*, *before*, *when*, and *if*. In this section, you are going to learn how to write complex sentences with the connector *because*.

Answering Questions with *Because*

How would you answer this question: *Why did you decide to study English?*
One popular way to answer a *why* question is to use the word *because* in the answer.

I am studying English <u>because</u> I wanted to learn a second language.

I am studying English <u>because</u> I want to study in an English-speaking country.

I am studying English <u>because</u> I like the way it sounds.

Notice how these sentences are organized. The first part of each sentence contains part of the question. It is then followed by *because*. The word *because* is followed by the reason (answer). Each example sentence has two clauses. Remember a clause has a subject and a verb. In formal writing, a clause with *because* must be part of a complex sentence.

If your sentence has *because* and one subject and verb only, the sentence is incorrect—it is a fragment. Fragments are not correct in formal writing. Study the following sentences.

Incorrect:	We didn't go to the beach. Because it was raining.
	(fragment)
Correct:	We didn't go to the beach because it was raining.
	(complex sentence)
Incorrect:	Megan is going to the disco. Because she likes to dance.
	(fragment)
Correct:	Megan is going to the disco because she likes to dance.
	(complex sentence)

NOTE: *Because* can also be used at the beginning of a sentence. When it is, you must put a comma at the end of the clause.

Incorrect:	Because they like to exercise Steve and Ken are going to the gym.
Correct:	Because they like to exercise, Steve and Ken are going to the gym.

Activity 11   Sentence or Fragment?

Read each group of words. If it is a fragment, write F on the line. If it is a complete sentence, write S on the line and add correct capitalization and punctuation. The first two have been done for you.

1. _____S_____ ~~d~~ante passed the test because he studied hard.

2. _____F_____ because the test has 50 questions

3. _____ because it was raining we didn't go to the beach

4. _____ because everyone had a wonderful time at the party

5. _____ she arrived late because her car broke down

6. _____ because he played poorly in the last match

7. _____ because I live in new york I go to the theater on broadway often

8. _____ because some committee members did not attend the conference

9. _____ the computers were down today because a storm knocked out the power

10. _____ we are going to postpone the meeting because the managers are out of the office

Activity 12   Using *Because* to Answer a Question

Answer the following questions using because *in your answer. Write complete sentences. The first one has been done for you.*

1. Why are you studying English?

   I am studying English because I want to enter Cornell University next year.

2. Why is soccer a popular sport?

   _____

3. Why is fast food popular in the United States?

   _____

4. Why do you like your hobby?

   _____

5. Why do some people like to drive fast?

   _____

6. Why are you using this book?

   _____

7. Why do you write letters to your family?

   _____

8. Why do some people eat breakfast in the morning?

   _____

9. Why do children learn to print before they learn cursive writing?

   _____

10. Why is hip-hop music popular?

    _____

WRITER'S NOTE: Use Commas Between Words in a List

The comma (,) is one of the most important marks of punctuation in English sentences. Commas help to make the meaning of sentences clear.

Sometimes good writers write sentences that contain a list of three or more things. Here are some examples.

ITEM 1   ITEM 2   ITEM 3   ITEM 4
Jennifer will visit London, Paris, Rome, and Prague next year. (list of nouns)

ITEM 1   ITEM 2   ITEM 3
Andrea is going to grow pink, yellow, and white roses in her garden. (list of adjectives)

You must put a comma after each item in the list except the last one. In addition, try to keep the words the same part of speech. For example, if you have three words, all three words should be nouns (or verbs or adjectives). The point is not to mix up the kinds of words.

(See Appendix 14 on page 231 for more comma rules.)

Activity 13   **Practicing Comma Rules**

For each item, combine the sentences into one sentence. Remember the comma rules that you have practiced for compound sentences, complex sentences, and lists. You may have to change or delete some words. The first one has been done for you.

1. I bought a new shirt and skirt at the mall. I got a winter coat.

   I bought a new shirt, skirt, and winter coat at the mall.

2. Michael likes to play soccer. He likes to play hockey and football.

   _____

   _____

   _____

3. My friend Rick is tall. He is strong and handsome.

   _____

   _____

   _____

4. John wants to go to the movies. Robert and Theo want to go, too.

    _____

    _____

    _____

5. I am going to bring sunglasses and a towel to the beach tomorrow. I am also going to bring a cold

    drink and a book.

    _____

    _____

    _____

6. At the dance, we ate food. We danced, and we played games.

    _____

    _____

    _____

7. In Moscow, Candice is going to visit the Kremlin and St. Basil's Cathedral. She is going to go to

    Gorky Park.

    _____

    _____

    _____

8. Ron and Harry rode the Ferris wheel at the fair. Elizabeth rode the Ferris wheel.

    _____

    _____

    _____

Editing

A

| Activity 14 | **Editing: Grammar and Sentence Review** |

Read the following paragraph. There are ten errors in the paragraph. Find and correct them. If you need help finding the errors, look at the numbers in parentheses on the left side of the paragraph. This number tells you how many errors are on each line. The first one has been done for you.

Paragraph 56

My Winter Vacation

My winter vacation is going to be wonderful because I am going to go to

(2) ~~m~~ontreal. I am going to go with my best friend. We going to spend two weeks
       M

(1) there, and it is going to be a wonderful time. I have the aunt who lives there,

(3) and she going to show us all the sights beautiful. We don't speak french very

(2) well so we are a little bit nervous. After I arrive in Canada I am going to buy a

(2) lot of souvenirs for my parents brother and friends. I can't wait for my vacation

      to begin!

Word Build•ing (wûrd bĭl′dĭng) *n.*

Activity 15 | **Word Building**

Study the following word forms. In the sentences on the right, choose the best word and write it in the blank space. Be sure to use the correct form of the verb. (Note: The word in bold is the original word that appears in the unit.)

Noun	Verb	Adjective	Sentence Practice
anger	anger	**angry**	1. She is going to be _____ when I tell her the news.
			2. The children _____ their mother yesterday.
honesty	Ø	honest	3. _____ is the best policy.
			4. Please give me an _____ answer.
nerve/nervou**ness**	Ø	**nervous**	5. Bill was _____ about taking the exam.
			6. I can see the _____ in her expression.
formal**ity**	Ø	formal	7. The dance next week is going to be _____.
			8. Meeting the new university president is only
			a _____.
uniqu**eness**	Ø	**unique**	9. Charmaine's style of dress is _____.
			10. The _____ of the Hungarian language
			makes it difficult to learn.

Noun endings: -y

Building Better Sentences

Correct and varied sentence structure is essential to the quality of your writing.
For further practice, go to Practice 6 on pages 240–241 in Appendix 16.

Activity 16	Original Writing Practice

Reread the paragraph on Carmen Viera in Activity 5 on page 141. Then review your answers to Activity 6 on pages 143–144. Use the information from Activity 6 to write about an event that is going to happen to you in the future.

Then follow these steps for writing and use the checklist. Put a check (✓) next to each step as you complete it. You may want to review What Is a Paragraph? in Unit 2 on page 42.

Step 1 _____ In your first sentence, tell who you are and what you are going to do in the future.

Step 2 _____ In the next two sentences, give more details to describe what you are going to do.

Step 3 _____ In the next four or five sentences, describe how you are going to complete this thing.

Step 4 _____ In the last sentence, tell why it is important for you to do this thing. (Use the word *because* in the final sentence.)

Step 5 _____ Try to use time words such as *after* and *as soon as* in some of your sentences in Step 3.

Step 6 _____ Try to include a list of three or more items in one of the sentences in Step 3. Remember the comma rule!

Step 7 _____ Write at least one compound and one complex sentence in your paragraph.

Checklist

✔ 1. ❑ Did you use *be going to* or *will* when you talked about the future?

✔ 2. ❑ Make sure that you use articles correctly in your sentences.

✔ 3. ❑ Make sure that you use commas correctly.

✔ 4. ❑ Make sure every sentence has a subject and a verb—no fragments!

✔ 5. ❑ Create a title for your paragraph.

Activity 17 **Peer Editing**

Choose someone that you work well with. Exchange papers from Activity 16 with that student. Read your partner's paragraph. Use Peer Editing Sheet 6 on page 263 to help you talk about your partner's work.

Activity 18 **Journal Writing**

EXTRA WRITING

Here are ten ideas for journal writing. Choose one or more of them to write about. Follow your teacher's directions. (We recommend that you skip a line after each line that you write. This gives your teacher a place to write comments.)

1. Write about something that you plan to do in the next two weeks. Include the people who are going to be with you, where you are going to be, and why you are going to do this.

2. Write about something that you plan to do in the next six months. Be sure to include where this activity is going to happen, who is going to be with you, and why you chose this activity.

3. Choose a current topic in the news. Read about it. Then write about what you think will happen and tell why.

4. Write about one of your goals. Include what the goal is, why this goal is important to you, and how long it is going to take to achieve.

5. Write about what you are going to do before you return home today. Make a list: Who are you going to be with? Are you going to do this thing for work, school, or pleasure? How long is it going to take you to complete these things?

6. Describe what your wedding will be like. How big will the wedding party be? Who will be there? Where will it happen?

7. Describe the job you want to have when you finish school. What kind of job is it? What are your responsibilities going to be in this job? Are you going to work for a company or by yourself? How much money are you going to earn in this job?

8. Write about what you plan to study (your major) in college. Why did you choose this subject? What classes are going to be easy for you, and what classes are going to be difficult? How long is it going to take you to get your degree?

9. Describe what life is going to be like in the year 2050. What new things are going to be available? How is life going to be better than it is now? How is life going to be worse than it is now?

10. Write about the future of space travel. What planets are humans going to visit? What things are going to be discovered in space?

MORE WRITING

For extra writing practice, see the activities in Unit 8, Appendix 17, and the *Great Sentences* website: http://esl.college.hmco.com/students.

Writing Sentences with Adjective Clauses and Place Phrases

GOAL: To learn how to write sentences with adjective clauses and place phrases

GRAMMAR AND SENTENCE STRUCTURE: Place phrases; modals

SENTENCE DEVELOPMENT: Sentences with adjective clauses

WRITING WITH ADJECTIVE CLAUSES

A paragraph usually contains several sentences. It is important that the sentences have variety. If they do not, your paragraph can be boring to read. You have already learned some things about sentence variety. You learned about compound sentences in Units 3–5 and complex sentences in Unit 6. In this unit, you will learn about sentences with adjective clauses.

RECOGNIZING SENTENCE VARIETY

Each of the following paragraphs contains similar information about tennis terms. However, one of the paragraphs sounds better than the other two. Read the three paragraphs. Which one do you think is best? Why?

Paragraph 57

Tennis Terms

Example 1

Tennis has many special terms. Most people do not know what these terms mean. One special word is *love*. In tennis *love* means "nothing" or "zero." Another word is *deuce*. *Deuce* is a special term. Deuce means the score is tied at three points for each player. Another term is *volley*. A volley is a shot. Usually a player runs to the net to try to end the point. The player hits the ball before it touches the ground. *Love, deuce,* and *volley* are special words. (86 words, 12 sentences)

Example 2

Tennis has many special terms. Tennis players understand these terms. Some people do not play tennis. Most of these people do not have any idea about the meaning of these terms. *Love* has a special meaning in tennis. For example, in tennis *love* means "nothing" or "zero." Another word is *deuce*. When tennis players use this word, it means each player has three points. In other words, deuce means the score is tied at three points for each player. Another term is *volley*. A volley is a shot. The player hits this shot before the ball touches the ground. Usually a player runs to the net to try to end the point. The player hits the ball before it touches the ground. *Love, deuce,* and *volley* are special words. All tennis players certainly know these words. (136 words, 16 sentences)

Example 3

Tennis has many special terms that tennis players know. Most people who do not play tennis do not understand the meaning of these terms. For example, one special word is *love*. In tennis, *love* means "nothing" or "zero." Another word that tennis players use is *deuce*. *Deuce* is a special term that means each player has three points. In other words, deuce means the score is tied at three points for each player. Another term that is used by tennis players is *volley*. A volley is a shot that the player hits before the ball touches the ground. Usually a player runs to the net to try to end the point. The player hits the ball before it touches the ground. *Love, deuce,* and *volley* are special words that all tennis players certainly know. (134 words, 12 sentences)

EVALUATING THE PARAGRAPHS

Example 1: Many sentences are short and choppy. The information does not flow smoothly or connect well. Here are some poor sentences from Example 1:

> *Deuce* is a special term.
>
> Another term is *volley*.
>
> A volley is a shot.

Example 2: This paragraph is better. For example, this complex sentence is an improvement:

> When tennis players use this word, it means each player has three points.

However, there are still a few short, choppy sentences. Some information is repeated in different sentences. Here are some poor sentences from Example 2:

Tennis has many special terms. Tennis players understand these terms.

Another term is *volley*. A volley is a shot.

Example 3: Did you think this is the best paragraph? Well, it is. The sentence combinations and variety are much better. Here are some good sentences from Example 3:

Deuce is a special term that means each player has three points.

Another term that is used by tennis players is *volley*.

A volley is a shot that the player hits before the ball touches the ground.

Combining Sentences with Adjective Clauses: *Who* and *That*

One way to combine two short sentences into a longer or better sentence is through the use of an adjective clause.

Reviewing Clauses

A clause is *any* group of words that includes a subject and a verb. (A sentence, for example, is a clause.) An adjective clause describes a noun. An adjective clause often begins with *who* or *that*.

NOTE: Use *who* in clauses that describe people. Use *that* in clauses that describe things.

Sentences with Adjective Clauses

Study these examples. Notice how the adjective clause comes *directly after* the noun it describes.

Two sentences: Joe bought a book. The book is very easy to read.

One sentence: Joe bought a book <u>that is very easy to read</u>.
ADJECTIVE CLAUSE

Two sentences: The teacher is Mrs. Habib. She cares about her students.

One sentence: The teacher <u>who cares about her students</u> is Mrs. Habib.
ADJECTIVE CLAUSE

On the Web
Try Unit 7
Activity 1
Activity 2
Activity 6

Activity 1 | **Practice with Adjective Clauses**

Write that *or* who *on the lines.*

Paragraph 58

On the Web
Try Unit 7
Activity 3

An Old Family Photo

This is an old photo of my family. In fact, this is a photo

(**1.**) _____ was taken about sixty years ago.

I remember the old sofa (**2.**) _____

was in my parents' living room. The two women

(**3.**) _____ are sitting on the sofa are

my mother and my grandmother. The woman

(**4.**) _____ has curly hair is my grandmother.

The woman (**5.**) _____ has long hair is my

mother. The little boy (**6.**) _____ is on the sofa

is Uncle Bob. The sofa in the picture is really old. In fact, this is the sofa (**7.**) _____

my grandmother received from her mother years before. The man (**8.**) _____ is

standing behind my grandmother is my grandfather. The two men (**9.**) _____ are

to the right of my grandfather are my father and Uncle Sam. The cat (**10.**) _____

you see under the sofa was my mother's pet. The name (**11.**) _____ my mother

gave her cat was Butterball because it was such a big, fat cat. This picture is so important to

me because all of the people (**12.**) _____ I love the most are in it. **Certainly** this

is a picture (**13.**) _____ I will **cherish** for many more years.

certainly: without a doubt; definitely   **cherish:** to treat with tenderness

WRITER'S NOTE: Use *Who* or *That* for People

Remember that adjective clauses that begin with *who* describe *people* only. Adjective clauses that begin with *that* can be for *people* or *things*. However, it is preferable to use *who* when you are describing people.

Incorrect:	I bought a cat who is white and brown.
Correct:	I bought a cat that is white and brown.
Acceptable:	Many people that watch basketball on TV also watch football.
Preferable:	Many people who watch basketball on TV also watch football.

Activity 2	**Adjective Clauses at the End of a Sentence**

In each item, combine the two sentences into one by using an adjective clause. Add the second sentence to the end of the first one, using who *or* that. *The first one has been done for you.*

1. The hula hoop is a toy. The hula hoop became popular in the 1960s.

   The hula hoop is a toy that became popular in the 1960s.

2. New Hampshire is a small state. New Hampshire is in the northeastern part of the United States.

3. Romansch is a language. Romansch comes from Latin.

4. Bolivia is a South American country. Bolivia does not have a coastline.

5. Nasi lemak is a Malaysian dish. Nasi lemak uses white rice and coconut milk.

_____

_____

_____

6. Dante Alighieri was an Italian writer. Dante Alighieri wrote *The Divine Comedy*.

_____

_____

_____

7. A meerkat is a rodent. It is a native of Africa.

_____

_____

_____

8. The *Titanic* was a ship. It sank in the North Atlantic Ocean.

_____

_____

_____

9. A coach is a person. A coach trains athletes to perform well in sports.

_____

_____

_____

10. El Prado is a famous museum. It is in the heart of Madrid, Spain.

_____

_____

_____

| Activity 3 | Sentence Combining: Adjective Clauses in the Middle of a Sentence |

In each item, combine the two sentences into one by using an adjective clause. Use the second piece of information in the middle of your new sentence. You will need to delete words from the second sentence. The first one has been done for you.

1. The food is called hummus. I like this food the best.

    The food that I like the best is hummus.
    _____

2. The movie was *Steel Magnolias*. We saw this movie on television last night.

    _____

3. The day was October 11. We arrived in Texas on this day.

    _____

4. The number was incorrect. Paul gave me this number.

    _____

5. The story was extremely interesting. Samir told this story.

    _____

6. The homework assignment was difficult. The grammar teacher gave us the homework assignment.

    _____

7. The man is my friend. The man is standing on the street corner.

    _____

8. The food got cold. We bought the food for dinner.

    _____

9. The police officer was very angry. The police officer gave me a speeding ticket.

    _____

10. The play is very popular in London. We are going to see this play tonight.

    _____

Activity 4   Identifying Adjective Clauses in a Paragraph

Read this paragraph and underline the three sentences that have adjective clauses.

Paragraph 59

A Possible Problem with the Schools

The school **district** in our city has a problem. The teachers who work in the city's schools say they might go on **strike**. The problem is money. The teachers want to go on strike because they get **salaries** that are very low. They say the salaries are not fair, so they want the school **officials** to **raise** teachers' salaries. There will be an emergency meeting of the school board this evening, and the public is invited. The teachers hope the people who attend the meeting will agree with them about the low salaries. Will the teachers go on strike? We are going to learn the answer to this question at tonight's meeting.

district: an official area or community   **officials:** directors, leaders

strike: to protest by not working   **raise:** to make higher

salary: money that a person earns

Activity 5   Examining Adjective Clauses

Look at the three sentences that you underlined in Activity 4. Copy each of them below. Then write the two short sentences that were combined to make the longer sentence.

Sentence 1: _____

     a. _____

     b. _____

Sentence 2: _____

     a. _____

     b. _____

     c. _____

Sentence 3: _____

     a. _____

     b. _____

| Activity 6 | Sentence Combining: Adjective Clauses |

Each paragraph is missing a sentence. Create the missing sentence from the sentences below the paragraph. Use all the ideas but not necessarily all the words. Your new sentence should have an adjective clause and be a good supporting sentence. Write your new sentence on the lines in the paragraph.

Paragraph 60

How the Weather Affects Me

Some people don't believe that the weather can **affect** the way you feel, but the weather certainly affects me. On rainy days, I feel like watching a movie or staying in bed. Rainy weather makes me **lazy**. It makes me want to stay inside and take it easy. When the weather is bright and sunny, I feel energetic. This kind of weather makes me want to go outside. I want to play tennis or go to the beach. When the temperature is cool and the sun is shining, I feel like working. I feel **productive**. _____

_____

As you can see, different kinds of weather have different effects on me.

affect: to change in some way   **lazy:** not active   **productive:** able to get things done

Missing sentence ideas: <u>This is the weather.</u>   +   <u>I like this weather the most.</u>

Paragraph 61

Some English Spelling Problems

Some English words are difficult to spell. One word that many people misspell is *receive*.

Receive is a problem because some people write the *i* before the *e*: *recieve*. The correct spelling

is *receive* with the *e* before the *i*. _____

_____

 Some people **confuse** *its* with *it's*. In addition, some people write the word *its* with an apostrophe:

its'. However, this last example is not an English word. Another example of bad spelling is

cemetery. Some people change the last *e* to *a* because of the pronunciation: *cemetary*. These are

just a few of the words that cause spelling problems for native and nonnative English speakers.

confuse: to mix without order   **cemetery**: a place where people are buried after they die

Missing sentence ideas: <u>Another word is the word *its*.</u> + <u>This word causes spelling</u>
<u>problems.</u>

GRAMMAR AND SENTENCE STRUCTURE:
Using Modals to Add Meaning

   Writers use modals to add extra information to the main verb in the sentence.
The modal comes before the main verb, and the main verb is always in base form.
Add *not* after the modal to make it negative. Each modal has a different meaning.
Below are some common modals, their meanings, and some example sentences.

will	to show the future	Next week Rachel **will travel** to the Ivory Coast.
should	to give advice	It is going to rain. You **should take** an umbrella
must	to show necessity	You **must have** a visa to visit that country.
might	to show possibility	The weather is good. We **might go** to the beach.
can	to show ability	Roberto **can speak** three languages.

   Remember, you cannot use two modals together. For example:

   Incorrect: We might can go to a new restaurant for dinner.
   Correct: We might go to a new restaurant for dinner.

Do not use the word *to* between the modal and the verb.

Incorrect:	We might to play football tomorrow.
Correct:	We might play football tomorrow.

Incorrect:	Can you to help us with this electricity bill?
Correct:	Can you help us with this electricity bill?

It is easy to make questions with modals.

Yes/No Questions

On the Web
Try Unit 7
Activity 6

Modal   +   Subject   +   Main Verb   +   Complement

Will you stop at the store for me?

Should I call my parents tonight?

Must we go to the party? (formal and implies a complaint)

Can they drive us to work?

NOTE: Might is rarely used in question form in American English.

WH- Questions about the Subject of the Sentence

Who will return the books?

Who should pay for the damage?

What punctuation must come at the end of a question?

Who can help us?

WH- Questions about the Rest of the Sentence

WH-Word + Modal + Subject + Main Verb + Complement

When will they finish the project?

Where should we go for dinner?

When can you meet me?

Activity 7   **Using Modals**

Answer the following questions about cooking a dinner for your friends. Use either should, must, might, can, *or* will.

1. What should you do before your friends arrive at your house?

_____

2. What must you do to the food before dinner?

   _____

3. What can your friends do for the dinner?

   _____

4. What might you cook if there are twenty guests?

   _____

5. What will you and your friends do after dinner tonight?

   _____

| Activity 8 | **Choosing the Best Modal** |

Read the following paragraph. Circle the modal that best completes the sentence. Sometimes both answers are correct. Be prepared to explain your answer.

Paragraph 62

Improve Your English More Quickly

Here is some good advice on how to improve your English more quickly. First, you
(**1.**) must / will always speak English. This requirement (**2.**) will / must help improve your
fluency. Second, you (**3.**) should / can also make friends with a native speaker. Then you
(**4.**) can / must talk to your new friend in English all the time. They (**5.**) can / will also correct
your mistakes because they know the language well. Third, you (**6.**) should / might read a
lot in English. This will improve your vocabulary. Finally, you (**7.**) might / should keep a
daily journal. This (**8.**) must / will give you practice writing in English. These suggestions
(**9.**) should / must help your English get better more rapidly.

Editing

Activity 9   **Editing: Error Correction and Sequencing**

The sentences below have some errors in capitalization and punctuation. First, find and correct the errors in each sentence. After you have corrected the errors, put the sentences in the correct order (1 through 6). The first one has been done for you.

a. ____1____ S̶udan is a country that is in the northeastern part of ḁfrica.

b. _____ it is a large country with many different people

c. _____ in conclusion, different areas of this country have very different histories

d. _____ the people who live in the southern part of the country were independent for many years

e. _____ however, the people who live in the northern part of the country were under foreign control for long periods of time

f. _____ some of the countries that ruled this northern area were egypt rome turkey and britain

Activity 10   **Copying Sentences**

Copy the sentences from Activity 9 in correct paragraph form. Be sure to add a title.

_____

_____

_____

_____

_____

_____

_____

_____

_____

_____

UNDERSTANDING PLACE PHRASES

You learned that to make a sentence more interesting, it is important to add details such as adjectives and connectors. In Unit 6, you learned that *time words* can add variety to your sentences. Another way to give more information in a sentence is to add place phrases.

GRAMMAR AND SENTENCE STRUCTURE: Prepositional Phrases of Place

Prepositional phrases of place function as adverbs—they modify a verb. They tell *where*. Here are some examples.

at the picnic	on the little table	under the chair	next to the front door
at school	over my head	at home	near the stove

Notice that the phrases begin with small words such as *at*, *in*, and *on*. These words are called prepositions. (See Appendix 12 pages 226–228 for preposition rules.) Every preposition in a place phrase needs a noun or pronoun. This noun or pronoun is called the object of the preposition. The combination of the preposition and the object is called a prepositional phrase.

Parts of a Prepositional Phrase (Place)

preposition	article (a, an, the, some, any) OR demonstrative pronoun (this, that, these, those) OR possessive pronoun (my, your, her, etc.) OR quantifier (one, two, etc.) OR Ø	adjective	noun OR pronoun	prepositional phrase
at	the		picnic	at the picnic
at			school	at school
on	the	little	table	on the little table
next to	the	front	door	next to the front door

It is common to put place phrases at the end of a sentence.

Incorrect: We ate <u>at the picnic</u> lots of hot dogs and hamburgers.

Correct: We ate lots of hot dogs and hamburgers <u>at the picnic</u>.

| Incorrect: | Loretta <u>in my house</u> lives. |
| Correct: | Loretta lives <u>in my house</u>. |

Place Phrases and Time Words

In sentences where you have a place phrase and a time word or phrase, remember this rule.

At the end of a sentence, place phrases usually come *before* time words or phrases.

Incorrect: Meet me <u>tomorrow afternoon</u> <u>in the backyard</u>.
                     TIME WORDS   PLACE PHRASE

Correct: Meet me <u>in the backyard</u> <u>tomorrow afternoon</u>.
                     PLACE PHRASE   TIME WORDS

Incorrect: She saw him <u>at 8 P.M.</u> <u>at the bank</u>.
                              ADV. TIME   ADV. PLACE

Correct: She saw him <u>at the bank</u> <u>at 8 P.M.</u>
                              ADV. PLACE   ADV. TIME

Correct: <u>At 8 P.M.</u>, she saw him <u>at the bank</u>.
              ADV. TIME   ADV. PLACE

Activity 11   Practicing with Place Phrases and Time Words

Read the sentence parts below. Put the parts in the correct order. Then write the complete sentences in the lines provided. You may have to add articles or verbs to the phrases. The first one has been done for you.

On the Web
Try Unit 7
Activity 4
Activity 5

1. Lucinda / in ten minutes / going to / drive to / video store

   <u>Lucinda is going to drive to the video store in ten minutes.</u>

2. last week / the Johnson sisters / party / excellent / have

   _____

   _____

3. next Monday / new car / we / buy

   _____

   _____

4. at gym / exercise / Janie / every morning

_____

_____

5. did you take / yesterday morning / in Mrs. Smith's class / grammar test

_____

_____ ?

6. leave / I / last night / my books / in car

_____

_____

7. two days ago / met Luis / they / at restaurant

_____

_____

8. Sara / the pie / right now / put / in oven

_____

_____

9. at airport / in ten minutes / our friends / arrive

_____

_____

10. squirrels / every day / nuts / bury / under our oak tree

_____

_____

Activity 12 | Practicing Adverbs of Place and Time Words

WWW

On the Web
Try Unit 7
Activity 5

Read the paragraph. It is missing three sentences. Below the paragraph are the missing sentences. Put the words in each sentence in the correct order. Then write the complete sentences in the spaces provided. You will have to add articles and use the correct verb tense.

Paragraph 63

A Long Flight

(**1.**) _____

_____

However, Daniel lives in La Paz, Bolivia, so he must take an airplane to Turkey before the

meeting. Daniel is going to go to the airport today. (**2.**) _____

_____

Because Daniel is going to take an international flight, he has to be at the airport at 3:00 P.M. If

he doesn't leave his house by noon, he is going to be late. It is almost 11:30 now. (**3.**) _____

_____

_____

Then he will leave on his long trip.

1. attend / in Istanbul, Turkey / Daniel / important company meeting / in two days
2. his flight / at 5:00 P.M. / leave / from Gate 32
3. his suitcase / Daniel / put / in ten minutes / in the car

Activity 13 | Sentence or Fragment Review

Read each group of words. If it is a fragment, write F on the line. If it is a complete sentence or question, write S on the line. The first two have been done for you.

1. ___F___ Every year go to the beach in Hawaii.

2. ___S___ Johnny has an appointment with a chiropractor at 4:30 P.M.

3. _____ We are going to have a big party to celebrate Mark's next birthday.

4. _____ Ten years to become a medical doctor in the United States.

5. _____ Next Tuesday am going to see the new Steven Spielberg film.

6. _____ Did you get a nice gift for your birthday last week?

7. _____ Wendy is eating lunch and talking to her friends in the cafeteria right now.

8. _____ Because the concert didn't end at 10 P.M.

9. _____ Peru and Argentina Spanish-speaking countries in the Southern Hemisphere.

10. _____ Ralph left his wallet at his friend's house last night.

Editing

Activity 14 — Editing: Grammar and Sentence Review

Read the following paragraph. It contains ten mistakes: adjective clauses (1), fragments (1), word order-adjectives (1), possessive adjectives (1), commas (2), articles (1), compound sentences (1), and capitalization (2). Find and correct the mistakes. The first one has been done for you.

**On the Web
Try Unit 7
Activity 7**

Paragraph 64

Visiting a New Country

There are m
~~M~~any reasons to visit a new country. First, you can see beautiful interesting and distant

places. For example, you can visit a Kremlin and Red Square in moscow. Another reason to travel

is to eat new types of food. If you visit Thailand, you can drink jasmine tea, you can eat

coconut-flavored rice. Finally, you can meet new people which live in these exotic countries. you

can talk to people and learn more about his likes and dislikes. As you can see, traveling to

another country is important for reasons different.

Word Build•ing (wûrd bǐl'dǐng) n.

Activity 15   **Word Building**

Study the following word forms. In the sentences on the right, choose the best word and write it in the blank space. Be sure to use the correct form of the verb. (Note: The word in bold is the original word that appears in the unit.)

Noun	Verb	Adjective	Sentence Practice
assignment	assign	Ø	1. Yesterday's _____ was very easy.
			2. My professor _____ too much homework last night.
energy	energize	**energetic**	3. Carla's cat is very _____.
			4. It has a lot of _____.
pronunciation	pronounce	Ø	5. Can you _____ the word "psychology"?
			6. Lee's _____ needs work.
confusion	**confuse**	confused/confusing	7. There was a lot of _____ at the concert.
			8. The directions for the test were _____.
decision	decide	decisive	9. The president _____ to run for re-election last week.
			10. Bindu made a _____ to drop out of college.

Noun endings: -sion
Adjective endings: -etic, -ed, -ing, -ive
Verb endings: -ize

Building Better Sentences

Correct and varied sentence structure is essential to the quality of your writing. For further practice, go to Practice 7 on page 241 in Appendix 16.

Activity 16   **Original Writing Practice**

In your opinion, which is better—cooking and eating food at home or eating out in a restaurant? Write a paragraph in which you answer this question and tell why.

Then follow these steps for writing, and use the checklist. Put a check (✓) next to each step as you complete it. You may want to review What Is a Paragraph? in Unit 2 on page 42.

Step 1 _____ In your first sentence, tell which type of food you prefer.

Step 2 _____ In the supporting sentences, give two or three reasons why you prefer this type of food.

Step 3 _____ Give details for each reason you give.

Step 4 _____ In the last sentence, summarize your opinion about the type of food that you prefer.

Step 5 _____ Write at least two adjective clauses.

Step 6 _____ Try to include time words and place phrases in some of the sentences in Step 2 or Step 3.

Step 7 _____ Write at least one compound and one complex sentence in Step 2 or Step 3.

Checklist

✔1. ❑ Did you use simple present tense in your paragraph?

✔2. ❑ Make sure that you use articles correctly.

✔3. ❑ Check for correct punctuation.

✔4. ❑ Make sure every sentence has a subject and a verb—no fragments!

✔5. ❑ Create a title for your paragraph.

Activity 17 | **Peer Editing**

Choose someone that you work well with. Exchange papers from Activity 16 with that student. Read your partner's paragraph. Use Peer Editing Sheet 7 on page 265 to help you talk about your partner's work.

Activity 18 | **Journal Writing**

EXTRA WRITING

Here are ten ideas for journal writing. Choose one or more of them to write about. Follow your teacher's directions. (We recommend that you skip a line after each line that you write. This gives your teacher a place to write comments.)

1. Write about an animal that you like. Describe the animal, tell where the animal lives, and tell why you like this animal so much.

2. Write about your dream house or apartment. Describe what this house looks like (how many rooms, what type of architecture, etc.). Write about the location of the house (in the mountains? on the beach? in a big city?).

3. Organized sports in school help children grow up to become better adults. Do you agree or disagree with this statement? Why?

4. Do you think that young children who know something about computers have an advantage in school today? Why or why not?

5. What is the worst decision that you ever made? Give details about why it was a bad decision.

6. What is the best decision that you ever made? Why was it a good decision? Did you come to this decision by yourself? How did you feel after you made this decision?

7. Write about a book that you like. Describe the book, briefly tell what happens in the story, and tell why you like this book.

8. Describe a painting that you like. Who painted it? What is in the painting? Describe colors. What do you feel when you look at the painting?

9. Describe your favorite kind of shopping. Where do you shop? What do you shop for? What do you like about the experience?

10. Describe your favorite place to visit. Where is this place? When do you go there? Why do you go there?

MORE WRITING

For extra writing practice, see the activities in Unit 8, Appendix 17, and the *Great Sentences* website: http://esl.college.hmco.com/students.

More Practice with Sentences and Paragraphs

GOAL: To practice sentence and paragraph skills from Units 1–7

PRACTICE WITH SENTENCES AND PARAGRAPHS

This unit contains twenty-five activities for practicing writing great sentences in great paragraphs. Some activities focus on sentences while others focus on paragraphs.

When you write the paragraphs in this unit, keep these things in mind:

Important Parts of a Paragraph

TOPIC SENTENCE	1. A good paragraph has a topic sentence that states the main idea.
Only ONE TOPIC	2. All of the sentences in the paragraph are about one topic.
INDENTED line	3. The first line of a paragraph is indented.
BODY AND SUPPORTING SENTENCES	4. A good paragraph has a sufficient number of supporting sentences.
CONCLUDING SENTENCE	5. The last sentence, or concluding sentence, brings the paragraph to a logical conclusion.

Practice 1

Basic Punctuation and Capitalization

Read each set of sentences. Correct the punctuation and capitalization errors. Then number the sentences in the correct order. Rewrite the sentences in paragraph form on the lines below. Finally, add a title.

1.

a. _____ in fact, the andes affect almost every aspect of peruvian life

b. _____ it is located in the south-central part of the continent

c. _____ peru is a country in south America

d. _____ the andes mountains run through the middle of the country

e. _____ the mountains affect weather agriculture and transportation

Paragraph 65

_____

_____

_____

_____

_____

_____

_____

_____

_____

2.

    a. _____ they are classified as birds but they cannot fly

    b. _____ instead, they are excellent swimmers because they have wings shaped
           like flippers

    c. _____ they live only in the cold regions in the southern hemisphere

    d. _____ penguins are very interesting animals

    e. _____ many people think that these birds live at the north pole but they
           do not

Paragraph 66

_____

_____

_____

_____

_____

_____

_____

_____

_____

_____

_____

Practice 2	**Word Forms**

This activity will help you practice correct noun and adjective forms, verb tense, and article usage. Read the paragraph. Underline the word that correctly completes each sentence.

On the Web
Try Unit 8
Activity 2

Paragraph 67

The Tomato: Fruit or Vegetable?

In supermarkets, people can find tomatoes in the vegetable section, but this common food is actually a (**1.** fruit / fruits). Many people (**2.** believe / believes) it is a (**3.** vegetable because / vegetable. Because) we eat it with (**4.** others / other) salty foods. For example, we eat

(**5.** tomato / tomatoes) in a salad or on sandwiches. We don't eat (**6.** tomato / tomatoes) for dessert or with anything sweet. However, the tomato is (**7.** really a / a really) fruit. Now isn't that strange?

Practice 3   **Editing in Four Steps**

Read this paragraph. Then rewrite it according to the four editing steps below.

Paragraph 68

EXAMPLE PARAGRAPH

Our Family's Koi Pond

Today my father is going to build a koi pond in our backyard. First, he is going to dig a big hole in the center of the yard. Then he is going to lay a sheet of black plastic in the hole. Next, he is going to put rocks around the edge of the hole. After that, he is going to fill the new pond with water. Finally, he is going to add plants and fish. It is going to be a lot of hard work, but he is going to enjoy it.

Make the following changes to the paragraph above. Write your new paragraph on the lines below.

Step 1. In the first sentence, change *my father* to *my father and I*.

Step 2. Change all the pronouns to fit the new subject.

Step 3. In the first sentence, change the word *Today* to *Last Saturday*.

Step 4. Change all the future tense verbs to past tense verbs.

Our Family's Koi Pond

_____

_____

_____

_____

_____

_____

_____

_____

Practice 4	**Editing in Five Steps**

Read this paragraph. Then rewrite it according to the five editing steps below.

Paragraph 69

EXAMPLE PARAGRAPH

Our First Garden

Two years ago, my brother and I planted our first garden. First, we chose the location of the garden. We put it in a place that gets a lot of sunlight. Then we dug up the ground. After that, we added fertilizer. Next, we took seeds and planted them in rows in the garden. Finally, we watered the new garden. It was hard work, but we are proud of our garden.

Make the following changes to the paragraph above. Write your new paragraph on the lines below.

Step 1. In the first sentence, change *my brother and I* to *Antonio*.

Step 2. Change all the pronouns and possessive words to fit the new subject.

Step 3. In the first sentence, change the phrase *Two years ago* to *Tomorrow*.

Step 4. Change all the past tense verbs to future tense verbs (*be going to*).

Step 5. Check the other verbs to make sure that they are correct.

Antonio's First Garden

_____

_____

_____

_____

_____

_____

_____

_____

Practice 5	**Verb Forms**

This activity will help you practice choosing the correct verb tense. Read the paragraph. Underline the correct verbs. Then answer the questions that follow the paragraph.

Paragraph 70

An Important Invention

I (**1.** believe / believed) that the light bulb is one of the most important inventions in the world. In the past, people (**2.** used / are using) candles to see at night. This light was very weak and difficult to see with. However, the light bulb now (**3.** allowed / allows) us to see things easily in the dark. This invention also (**4.** help / helps) us to do more work in one day. Before the light bulb, most work (**5.** ends / ended) at sundown. Now people can continue to work outdoors or in their offices for much longer at night. In addition, people can do more fun things when it is dark. For example, sports fans (**6.** watch / watched) baseball games at night on lighted fields. Music lovers (**7.** listen / are listening) to a concert in a lighted stadium. Without the light bulb, people would not have as many choices for work or play.

1. What is the topic sentence of the paragraph?

   _____

   _____

2. How many sentences does the paragraph have? _____

3. What reasons does the writer give to support the main idea?

   _____

   _____

4. What two verb tenses does the writer use? Why?

   _____

   _____

Practice 6	**Original Writing Practice with Verb Tenses**

In Practice 5, you read about one writer's opinion about an important invention in history. What do you think is an important invention in history? Write a short paragraph about it. Include a topic sentence and three examples to support your opinion. Create a title for your paragraph.

_____

_____

_____

_____

_____

_____

_____

Practice 7	**Verb Tense**

This activity will help you practice choosing the correct verb tense. Read the paragraph. Underline the correct verbs. Then answer the questions that follow the paragraph.

Paragraph 71

**On the Web
Try Unit 8
Activity 4**

A Busy Day

Tomorrow (**1.** is / is going to be) a busy day for me. Usually, I (**2.** get / am getting) up at seven o'clock in the morning. However, tomorrow I (**3.** get / am going to get) up at five o'clock because I am going to go to the gym. After I finish at the gym, I (**4.** go / am going to go) to work. I usually (**5.** start / am starting) work at nine o'clock. Tomorrow I (**6.** start / am going to start) work at eight o'clock. After work, I frequently (**7.** have / am having) dinner with my friends. However, tomorrow I (**8.** go / will go) directly to my mother's house because it is her birthday. We (**9.** have / are going to have) a big party for her. I know I will have a lot of fun tomorrow.

1. What is the topic sentence of the paragraph?

   _____

   _____

2. How many sentences does the paragraph have? _____

3. What reasons does the writer give to support the main idea?

   _____

   _____

4. What two tenses does the writer use? Why?

   _____

   _____

| Practice 8 | Original Writing Practice with Verb Tense |

In Practice 7, you read about one person's busy day. Write a paragraph describing a busy day in your life. It can be about a day in the past, present, or future. Include a topic sentence and three examples to support your opinion. Create a title for your work.

                              _____

_____

_____

_____

_____

_____

_____

Practice 9   **Articles**

This activity will help you review the correct use of articles. Read the paragraph. Underline the article that correctly completes each sentence. (Note: ø means "no article.")

Paragraph 72

Shark!

I'll never forget my first encounter with (**1.** a / an / ø) shark. I was sixteen, and I was visiting Australia with my family. My father and I went scuba diving on (**2.** a / the / ø) Great Barrier Reef. We went out to (**3.** a / the / ø) reef with many other tourists on (**4.** a / an / the) special boat. When we got to (**5.** a / the / ø) reef, the scuba diving instructor helped us put on our equipment. Then we dove into (**6.** a / the / ø) clear blue water. Everything was so beautiful! There were colorful fish and lots of different kinds of coral. I swam everywhere. Suddenly, I saw (**7.** a / an / the) huge gray shark swim towards me. I looked around for my father, but I was far away from him and (**8.** a / an / the) group of tourists. What could I do? (**9.** A / An / The) shark got closer and closer. I was so scared that I couldn't move. Just when I thought that it might bite me, (**10.** a / an / the) shark turned and swam (**11.** a / the / ø) other way. Unbelievable! I quickly found my father. Now I never swim off by myself when I go scuba diving.

Editing

Practice 10   **Editing for Articles**

**On the Web
Try Unit 8
Activity 3**

Follow these instructions:

1. Reread your writing in Practice 6 and Practice 8.
2. Choose four sentences from your paragraphs that contain articles. Write them below.
3. Ask a partner to check your sentences. Did you use articles correctly?

_____

_____

_____

_____

_____

_____

_____

_____

WRITER'S NOTE: Add Interest to Your Writing

Remember to use a variety of sentence types (simple, compound, complex) in your writing. Different kinds of sentences will make your writing more interesting. You can also use adverbs and adjectives to add variety and interest to your writing.

| Practice II | **Connecting Sentences in a Paragraph** |

This activity will help you practice combining sentences with a connector. Combine each underlined pair of sentences. You may use and, but, *or* so *to connect them. Remember to add a comma before the connecting word. You may have to delete some words. Rewrite the paragraph on the next page.*

Paragraph 73

EXAMPLE PARAGRAPH

My First Car

My first car was the best car in the world. It was a Ford Mustang. (**1.**) <u>My Mustang was bright blue</u>. <u>It was very powerful</u>. All my friends were jealous when they saw it. (**2.**) <u>They wanted to drive it</u>. <u>I told them they could not</u>. I

said that they could be passengers or pedestrians. (**3.**) <u>My friends didn't want to walk</u>. <u>They always chose to be passengers</u>. However, the best thing about my car was the way it made me feel. (**4.**) <u>Every weekend I drove to the movie theater in that car</u>. <u>Every weekend my friends rode with me</u>. We felt like movie stars because everyone stared at us in the beautiful blue car. I will never forget the fun that I had in that cool car.

_____

_____

_____

_____

_____

_____

_____

_____

Editing

| Practice 12 | **Editing for Connectors (*and, but, so*)** |

Follow these instructions:

1. Reread your writing in Practice 6 and Practice 8. Did you use any connectors in your sentences?

2. If so, rewrite those sentences below.

3. If not, combine two of your sentences with a connector.

4. Ask a partner to check your sentences. Did you use the connectors correctly?

_____

_____

_____

_____

_____

| Practice 13 | **Adjective Clauses with *Who* and *That*** |

Read the paragraph. Underline the word that correctly completes each sentence.

Paragraph 74

www

**On the Web
Try Unit 8
Activity 5**

How the Months of the Year Got Their Names

The names of all twelve months come from Roman culture and myths. First, there are several months (**1.** that / who) are named after Roman gods and goddesses. The Roman god of beginnings (**2.** that / who) gave us the month of January is Janus. The month (**3.** that / who) got its name from the Roman god of war is March. May and June honor the Roman goddesses Maia and Juno. Some months get their names from festivals. Both February and April come from special celebrations (**4.** that / who) appeared on the old Roman calendar. Two months (**5.** that / who) come in the summer got their names from Roman emperors. July is the month (**6.** that / who) honors Julius Caesar, and August is named for Emperor Augustus. Finally, September, October, November, and December are named after the seventh, eighth, ninth, and tenth months of the Roman calendar. The month names (**7.** that / who) are so commonly used today certainly have a very rich history.

Editing

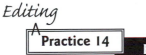

| Practice 14 | **Editing for Adjective Clauses** |

Follow these instructions:

1. Reread your writing in Practice 6 and Practice 8. Did you use adjective clauses in your writing?
2. If so, rewrite those sentences below.
3. If not, combine two of your sentences using an adjective clause.
4. Ask a partner to check your sentences. Did you use the adjective clauses correctly?

_____

_____

_____

_____

Practice 15   **Topic Sentences and Supporting Sentences**

This activity will help you recognize the difference between a topic sentence and supporting sentences. Each pair of sentences is about one topic. Decide which sentence is the topic sentence (T) and which is a supporting sentence (S). (Hint: The topic sentence gives more general information.)

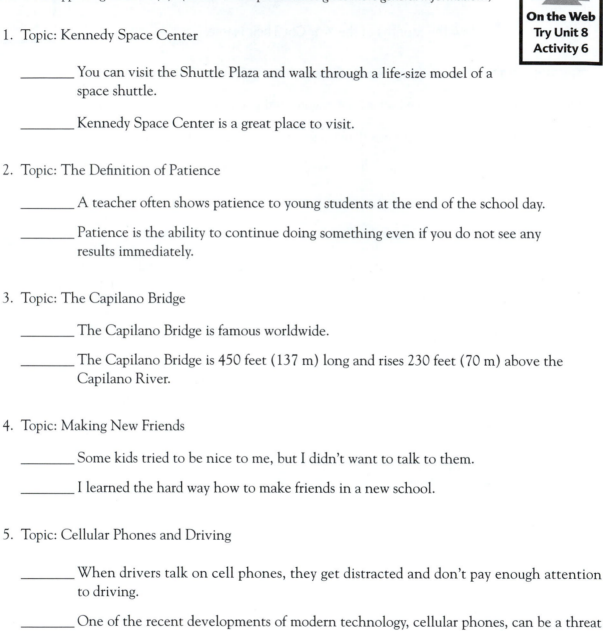

**On the Web
Try Unit 8
Activity 6**

1. Topic: Kennedy Space Center

    _____ You can visit the Shuttle Plaza and walk through a life-size model of a space shuttle.

    _____ Kennedy Space Center is a great place to visit.

2. Topic: The Definition of Patience

    _____ A teacher often shows patience to young students at the end of the school day.

    _____ Patience is the ability to continue doing something even if you do not see any results immediately.

3. Topic: The Capilano Bridge

    _____ The Capilano Bridge is famous worldwide.

    _____ The Capilano Bridge is 450 feet (137 m) long and rises 230 feet (70 m) above the Capilano River.

4. Topic: Making New Friends

    _____ Some kids tried to be nice to me, but I didn't want to talk to them.

    _____ I learned the hard way how to make friends in a new school.

5. Topic: Cellular Phones and Driving

    _____ When drivers talk on cell phones, they get distracted and don't pay enough attention to driving.

    _____ One of the recent developments of modern technology, cellular phones, can be a threat to safe driving.

Practice 16   **Sentence Order in Paragraphs**

On the Web
Try Unit 8
Activity 1

Read all the sentences below. Then put them in a logical paragraph order. When you finish, write the sentences in correct paragraph format on the lines below. Be sure to add an appropriate title.

a. _____ Instead, breakfast for them often consists of eggs with toast and coffee.

b. _____ People in Malaysia eat rice for breakfast, too, but their rice is cooked in coconut milk.

c. _____ Breakfast foods vary from country to country.

d. _____ However, people in most countries in Central and South America do not eat rice for breakfast.

e. _____ People eat this sweet, flavored rice with a red paste that is made of ground chili peppers and other ingredients.

f. _____ In Japan, for example, it is common to eat rice, soup, and fish for breakfast.

g. _____ From these varied breakfast items, it is clear that breakfast foods are different around the world.

Paragraph 75

_____

_____

_____

_____

_____

_____

_____

_____

_____

Practice 17 — Pre-reading Questions

Discuss the answers to these questions in a small group. Then read the paragraph.

1. Do you like to cook? If so, what is your favorite meal to prepare?
2. How much time do you spend in the kitchen?
3. Have you ever eaten linguine?

Paragraph 76

EXAMPLE PARAGRAPH

Something Easy to Cook

One of the quickest and easiest meals to prepare is linguine with tomato sauce. First, fill a large pot about three-quarters full with water. Bring the water to a boil and add about eight ounces of your favorite linguine. It will take about ten minutes for the pasta to cook thoroughly. While the pasta is cooking, heat a large skillet with about two tablespoons of olive oil. Slice three or four cloves of garlic and add them to the skillet. Stir frequently until the garlic cloves become a golden brown color. Add a large can of tomato sauce to the garlic and oil. Then add a pinch of salt and pepper. When the linguine is done, strain it in a colander and put the linguine in the skillet. Add some grated parmesan cheese and some chopped basil. Your delicious linguine dinner is ready. *Buon appetito!*

Practice 18 — Analyzing the Paragraph

Read each question about Paragraph 76 in Practice 17. Circle the best answer.

1. What is the main topic of the paragraph?
   a. The health benefits of linguine
   b. Why linguine is inexpensive
   c. Cooking a quick linguine meal

2. What is the topic sentence of this paragraph?
   a. One of the quickest and easiest meals to prepare is linguine with tomato sauce.
   b. First, fill a large pot about three-quarters full with water.
   c. Add some grated parmesan cheese and some chopped basil.

3. In your opinion, what does the paragraph explain?

    a. It explains why cooking linguine is better than eating fast food.

    b. It tells you that linguine is the easiest and most delicious food to make in the kitchen.

    c. It lists the steps necessary to make a quick linguine dinner.

4. How many (food) ingredients does the author mention in the paragraph?

    a. Three

    b. Eight

    c. Ten

5. Read the paragraph again. What verb tense is most often used?

    a. Simple past

    b. Simple present

    c. Future

WRITER'S NOTE: Words That Express an Opinion

When you write about your beliefs on a subject, you are giving your *opinion*. Here are some words that you can use when you write about your opinion:

believe	I *believe* that no one should smoke in public.
feel	I *feel* that smoking is a personal decision.
think	I *think* that smoking is bad for your health.
agree	I *agree* with the new laws that prohibit smoking.
disagree	I *disagree* with the new laws that prohibit smoking.
have mixed feelings	I *have mixed feelings* about smoking in public places. (This means the writer has more than one opinion on the topic and the opinions conflict with each other.)

**On the Web
Try Unit 8
Activity 7**

RESPONDING TO ISSUES IN THE NEWS

In the following section, you will read paragraphs that discuss topics in the news. You will also read people's opinions on these issues. Then you will write about your opinions.

Practice 19 | **Responding to a Reading Passage**

Read the following paragraph. Then read the opinions that follow and answer the questions.

Paragraph 77

EXAMPLE PARAGRAPH

Smoking in Public Places

In the late 1990s, several U.S. cities voted **to ban** smoking in restaurants and bars. The main reason for doing this was public health. The action was **controversial** because smokers felt **discriminated against**. Some **activists** believe that **barring** smokers from these public **establishments** is not the only solution to the problem. In fact, they propose establishing separate areas for smokers and nonsmokers, installing advanced ventilation systems, and using other measures. However, the **ruling** to ban smoking in public places is now a law.

to ban: to prohibit; to make illegal

controversial: causing conflict or debate

discriminated against: judged or acted upon unfavorably

activist: someone who works to support a political cause

barring: prohibiting; banning

establishment: business

ruling: decision

Opinion 1

Melinda:

Because second-hand smoke causes cancer, I believe that banning smoking in restaurants and bars is correct. If smoking is not allowed in buildings such as post offices and banks, why should it be any different for restaurants and bars? One day smoking is going to be against the law, so this is not going to be an issue anymore. Until then, the smokers must smoke outside.

1. What is the topic sentence of Melinda's paragraph?

_____

_____

2. In your own words, write one sentence about how Melinda feels about this issue.

_____

_____

3. What argument does Melinda use to support her opinion?

_____

_____

Opinion 2

Scott:

I'm not a smoker, but I disagree with the new laws that prohibit smoking. I think it's unfair to single out smokers and make them feel unaccepted. People in bars and restaurants can drink too much and possibly get into fatal car accidents, and that is much worse than smoking. I feel bad for smokers because they cannot smoke when they want to. I think that fewer smokers are going to go out to restaurants and bars because of this law.

1. What is the topic sentence of Scott's paragraph?

_____

_____

2. In your own words, write one sentence about how Scott feels about this issue.

_____

_____

3. What argument does Scott use to support his opinion?

_____

_____

Opinion 3

Amanda:

I really have mixed feelings about this new law. On the one hand, I'm glad that when I go into a bar my eyes don't burn from the cigarette smoke. Sometimes bars are so smoky that you cannot see one foot in front of you. On the other hand, I believe that there can be a compromise. I go to some restaurants with smoking and nonsmoking areas, and I have no problems there. Maybe the two groups can reach a compromise that will satisfy everyone.

1. What is the topic sentence of Amanda's paragraph?

_____

_____

2. In your own words, write one sentence about how Amanda feels about this issue.

_____

_____

3. How is Amanda's opinion different from Melinda's and Scott's?

_____

_____

WRITER'S NOTE: *Should* and the Tone of Verbs

You can use the word *should* to soften your verbs when you give your opinion. For example:

Strong:	People <u>must</u> not talk on their cellular phones in their cars.
Strong:	People <u>have to</u> stop talking on their cellular phones in their cars.
Softer:	People <u>should</u> not talk on their cellular phones in their cars.

Practice 20   Original Writing

Now it's your turn to state your opinion about this issue. Write a paragraph that tells if you support or oppose the idea of banning smoking in restaurants and bars. Indent your paragraph.

Careful! Be sure that the first sentence (the topic sentence) states your opinion. Include good supporting sentences. Give your paragraph a title.

_____

_____

_____

_____

_____

_____

_____

_____

_____

_____

_____

WRITER'S NOTE: Editing

Remember that it is very important to edit your writing. When you edit your writing, you find and correct your mistakes. You should also ask other people to edit your work. They may find mistakes that you missed.

Practice 21 — Peer Editing

Exchange papers from Practice 20 with another student. Read your partner's paragraph. Use Peer Editing Sheet 8 on page 267 to help you talk about your partner's work.

Practice 22 — Responding to a Reading Passage

Read the following paragraph. Then read the opinions that follow and answer the questions.

Paragraph 78

EXAMPLE PARAGRAPH

A Medical Dilemma

Recently, there was a **controversy** in Great Britain involving **conjoined twins**. A woman from Malta gave birth to baby girls. Unfortunately, these girls were attached to each other. The parents, who were strict Catholics, did not want doctors to separate the babies. They said it was murder. The doctors explained that with the operation, one baby would live. Without the operation, both babies would die. The British court made the final decision. The doctors performed the operation, and one of the babies died.

controversy: debate or conflict   conjoined twins: twins that are physically attached

Opinion 1

Joseph:

A court must not have more power over someone's children than the family. It is unbelievable that the court forced its decision on this unlucky family. The birth of these girls was a natural event, and it was destiny that they were born conjoined twins. The parents didn't want the operation because of their religion. That is a strong enough reason to let the parents make the final decision.

1. What is the topic sentence of Joseph's paragraph?

   _____

   _____

2. In your own words, write one sentence about how Joseph feels about this case.

   _____

   _____

3. What argument does Joseph use to support his idea?

   _____

   _____

Opinion 2

Rebecca:

When a human life is involved, the court must have some power in making the decision. Of course the case of these conjoined twin girls is a tragedy, but modern science could help them! The parents used their religion to make the decision. The court only wanted to save a human life. Maybe the parents didn't realize that both little girls would die without the operation. To save one baby, I agree with the court.

1. What is the topic sentence of Rebecca's paragraph?

   _____

   _____

2. In your own words, write one sentence about how Rebecca feels about this case.

_____

_____

3. What argument does Rebecca use to support her idea?

_____

_____

WRITER'S NOTE: Vary Your Vocabulary

   Vocabulary is a key part of good writing. Your level of vocabulary is an indication of your English proficiency. The reader's opinion of your writing will be higher if you use better vocabulary. Variety is important. In your paragraphs, try to use synonyms, phrases, and sometimes whole sentences to say the same information in a different way. Avoid using the same words all the time.

Word Build•ing (wûrd bĭl′dĭng) *n.*

| Practice 23 | Word Building |

Study the following word forms. In the sentences on the right, choose the best word and write it in the blank space. Be sure to use the correct form of the verb. (Note: The word in bold is the original word that appears in the unit.)

Noun	Verb	Adjective	Sentence Practice
transport<u>ation</u>	transport	Ø	1. New York City's public _____ is excellent.
			2. A truck driver _____ goods from one place to another.
swimm<u>ers</u>/swimm<u>ing</u>	swim	Ø	3. Do you like the sport of _____?
			4. _____ have very muscular bodies.

differ<u>ence</u>	differ	**different**	5. The twins _____ in their political views.
			6. There is a small _____ between British English and American English.
power	Ø	**power<u>ful</u>**	7. My car's engine doesn't have the _____ to drive up the mountain.
			8. Joann gave a very _____ speech.
disagree<u>ment</u>	**disagree**	disagree<u>able</u>	9. There was a _____ between the coach and his players.
			10. Many people _____ about the correct way to load a dishwasher.

Noun endings: -er
Adjective endings: -able

Practice 24	**Original Writing**

Now it's your turn to state your opinion about this case. Tell if you agree or not with what the court decided about the twins.

Careful! Be sure that the first sentence you write (topic sentence) states the opinion you agree with. Include good supporting sentences. Give your paragraph a title.

_____

_____

_____

_____

_____

_____

_____

_____

_____

_____

Practice 25   **Peer Editing**

Exchange papers from Practice 24 with another student. Read your partner's paragraph. Use Peer Editing Sheet 9 on page 269 to help you talk about your partner's work.

Appendixes

Definitions of Useful Language Terms

Adjective   A word that describes a noun.

Lexi is a very <u>smart</u> girl.

Adverb   A word that describes a verb or an adjective.

The secretary types <u>quickly</u>.

Article   The definite article is *the*. The indefinite articles are *a* and *an*.

<u>The</u> teacher gave <u>an</u> assignment to <u>the</u> students.

Jillian is eating <u>a</u> piece of cake.

Clause   A group of words that has a subject and a verb. Sentences can have one or more clauses.

<u>Roger</u> <u>wants</u> to go to Harvard University. (one clause)
SUBJECT   VERB

<u>Jeff</u> <u>needs</u> to write his report because <u>he</u> <u>wants</u> to pass the class.
SUBJ.   VERB   SUBJ. VERB
 (CLAUSE 1)   (CLAUSE 2)

Noun   A noun is a person, place, thing, or idea.

<u>Sandra</u> likes to eat <u>sandwiches</u> for <u>lunch</u>.

<u>Love</u> is a very strong <u>emotion</u>.

Object   A word that comes after a transitive verb or a preposition.

Jim bought a new <u>car</u>.

I left my jacket in the <u>house</u>.

Predicate   The part of the sentence that shows what the subject does.

<u>Mr. Johnston</u> <u>walked to the park</u>.
    SUBJECT   PREDICATE

<u>My neighbor's dog</u> <u>buried a bone in the yard</u>.
      SUBJECT   PREDICATE

Preposition   A word that can show location, time, and direction. Some common prepositions are *around, at, behind, between, from, on, in, near, to, over, under, with.*

Punctuation   Punctuation includes the period (.), comma (,), question mark (?), and exclamation point (!).

Subject   The subject of a sentence tells who or what the sentence is about.

My science teacher gave us a homework assignment. It was difficult.

Tense   A verb has tense. Tense shows when the action happened.

Simple present:	She walks to school every day.
Present progressive:	She is walking to school now.
Simple past:	She walked to school yesterday.
Past progressive:	She was walking to school when she saw her friend.
Future:	She is going to walk to school.

Verb   The word that shows the action of the sentence.

They speak French.

My father works at the power plant.

Review of Verb Tenses

Verb Tense	Affirmative	Negative	Usage
Present	I work you take he studies she does we play they have	I do not work you do not take he does not study she does not do we do not play they do not have	1. for actions that happen all the time 2. for facts
Past	I worked you took he studied she did we played they had	I did not work you did not take he did not study she did not do we did not play they did not have	1. for actions that are finished 2. for facts
Present Progressive	I am working you are taking he is studying she is doing we are playing they are having*	I am not working you are not taking he is not studying she is not doing we are not playing they are not having*	1. for actions that are happening now 2. for future actions if a future time adverb is used or understood
Future (Be going to)	I am going to work you are going to take he is going to study she is going to do we are going to play they are going to have	I am not going to work you are not going to take he is not going to study she is not going to do we are not going to play they are not going to have	1. for future actions

Verb Tense	Affirmative	Negative	Usage
Future (Will)	I will work you will take he will study she will do we will play they will have	I will not work you will not take he will not study she will not do we will not play they will not have	1. for future actions
Present Perfect	I have worked you have taken he has studied she has done we have played they have had	I have not worked you have not taken he has not studied she has not done we have not played they have not had	1. for actions that began in the past and continue until the present 2. for actions in the indefinite past time 3. for past actions that are interrupted by other actions or events
Past Progressive	I was working you were taking he was studying she was doing we were playing they were having*	I was not working you were not taking he was not studying she was not doing we were not playing they were not having*	1. for longer actions that are interrupted by other actions or events

*have can be used in progressive only when it has an active meaning in special expressions such as:

have a party

have a good time

have a bad time

have a baby

Capitalization Rules

1. The first word in a sentence or question is capitalized.

   Every week I go to the movies.

   Do you like to play tennis?

2. The pronoun *I* is always capitalized.

   Larry and I are brothers.

3. People's formal and professional titles use capital letters.

   Mr. and Mrs. Jenkins are on vacation.

   Lisa saw Dr. Johansen at the bank yesterday.

4. Proper names (specific people and places) use capital letters.

   The Coliseum in Rome is a beautiful old monument.

   Irene met her brother Don and his dog Skippy at the park.

5. Names of streets use capital letters.

   Ruth lives on Wilson Avenue.

6. Geographical locations (cities, states, countries, continents, lakes, and rivers) use capital letters.

   I am going to travel to London, England, next week.

   The Arno River passes through Tuscany, Italy.

7. The names of languages and nationalities use capital letters.

   My grandmother speaks Polish.

   Jessica is going to learn Japanese.

   Melisa is Venezuelan, but her husband is Cuban.

8. Most words in titles of paragraphs, essays, and books are capitalized. The first letter of a title is always capitalized, and the other important words in a title are capitalized. Do not capitalize prepositions (*to, in*), conjunctions (*and, but*), or articles (*a, an, the*) unless they are the first word of the title.

The Life of Billy Barnes

Crime and Punishment

The Catcher in the Rye

In the Bedroom

9. Specific course names are capitalized.

Are you taking History 101 at 10:00 A.M.?

Are you taking history this semester? (general subject—no capital letter)

APPENDIX 4

Spelling Rules for Regular Past Tense Verbs

1. Add *-ed* to the base form of most verbs.

   start   started
   finish   finished
   wash   washed

2. Add only *-d* when the base form ends in an *e*.

   live   lived
   care   cared
   die   died

3. If the verb ends in a consonant + *y*, change the *y* to *i* and add *-ed*.

   dry   dried
   carry   carried
   spy   spied

4. If the verb ends in a vowel + *y*, do not change the *y*. Just add *-ed*.

   pray   prayed
   stay   stayed
   destroy   destroyed

5. If the verb has one syllable and ends in a consonant + vowel + consonant (CVC), double the final consonant and add *-ed*.

   stop   stopped
   CVC

   rob   robbed
   CVC

6. Do not double final *w* or *x*.

sew	sewed
mix	mixed

7. If the verb has two syllables, and the final syllable is stressed, double the final consonant.

ad mit´	admitted
oc cur´	occurred
per mit´	permitted

8. If the verb has two syllables, and the final syllable is *not* stressed, do *not* double the final consonant.

hap´pen	happened
lis´ten	listened
o´pen	opened

Irregular Past Tense Verbs

These are some of the more common irregular verbs in English.

Base Form	Simple Past	Base Form	Simple Past
be (am/is/are)	was / were	fight	fought
bite	bit	find	found
bleed	bled	flee	fled
blow	blew	forget	forgot
break	broke	get	got
become	became	give	gave
begin	began	grow	grew
bring	brought	have	had
build	built	hear	heard
buy	bought	hide	hid
catch	caught	hit	hit
choose	chose	hold	held
come	came	hurt	hurt
cost	cost	keep	kept
cut	cut	know	knew
do	did	leave	left
drink	drank	let	let
drive	drove	lose	lost
eat	ate	make	made
fall	fell	pay	paid
feel	felt	put	put

Base Form	Simple Past	Base Form	Simple Past
read	read	stand	stood
run	ran	steal	stole
say	said	swim	swam
see	saw	take	took
sell	sold	teach	taught
send	sent	tell	told
set	set	think	thought
sing	sang	throw	threw
sit	sat	understand	understood
sleep	slept	wear	wore
speak	spoke	win	won
spend	spent	write	wrote

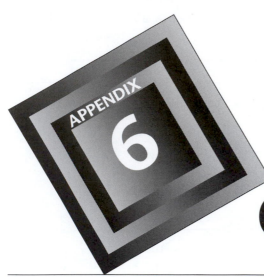

Spelling of the -*ing* (present participle) Form of Verbs

1. Add -*ing* to most verbs.

catch	catching
wear	wearing
go	going

2. If the verb ends with a consonant + *e*, drop the *e* and then add -*ing*.

write	writing
drive	driving
take	taking

3. If the verb has one syllable and ends with a consonant + a vowel + a consonant (CVC), double the final consonant.

run   running
CVC

sit   sitting
CVC

stop   stopping
  CVC

4. Do not double *w*, *x*, or *y*.

sew	sewing
mix	mixing
say	saying

5. If the verb has two syllables and the *last* syllable is stressed, double the final consonant.

be gin´	beginning
ad mit´	admitting
re fer´	referring

6. If the verb has two syllables and the first syllable is stressed, do *not* double the final consonant.

o´pen	opening
lis´ten	listening
frigh´ten	frightening

Common Stative, or Nonaction Verbs

Below is a list of common stative, or nonaction, verbs. In general, these verbs do not use the progressive tense because they do not show an action.

Incorrect: She is drinking that coffee because she is disliking green tea.

Correct: She is drinking that coffee because she <u>dislikes</u> green tea.

agree	hear	own	taste
be	know	prefer	think
believe	like	remember	understand
cost	love	see	want
dislike	mean	seem	
hate	need	smell	

Definite Article *The*

Use the article *the* when you are writing about a specific noun.

1. Use *the* for the second (and subsequent) time you write about something.
    I bought a new coat yesterday. The coat is blue and gray.

2. Use *the* when the writer and the reader both know about or are familiar with the subject.
    Are you going to the bank this afternoon?
    (Both the writer and the reader know which bank they are talking about.)

3. Use *the* when the noun you are referring to is unique (there is only one).
    The sun and the Earth are both in the Milky Way galaxy.
    The Eiffel Tower is a beautiful monument.

4. Use *the* with specific time periods.
    You must be very quiet for the next hour.

5. Use *the* when the other words in your sentence make the noun specific.
    The cat in the picture is very pretty. (*in the picture* tells which cat)

6. Do not use *the* before names or when you talk about something in general.
    Andrei Bulgakov is a famous Russian writer.
    Jason is going to make a doghouse with wood.

7. Some geographic locations require *the*, but others do not. Cities, states, countries, continents, and lakes do not use *the*.

Sylvie is from <u>Venezuela</u>. She lives near <u>Lake Maracaibo</u>.
COUNTRY NAME   LAKE NAME

However, if there is an *s* (plural) or the words *united, union, kingdom,* or *republic* in the name of the country, use *the*.

We are going to <u>the Bahamas</u> for our vacation. (The country name ends with *-s*.)

Who is the president of <u>the United States</u>? (*United* is in the country name.)

Most buildings, bodies of water (except lakes), mountain chains, and deserts use *the*.

<u>The White House</u> is in Washington, D.C.
BUILDING NAME

<u>The Amazon</u> is a very long river in South America.
RIVER NAME

<u>Lake Baikal</u> is a large fresh water lake in Russia.
LAKE NAME—NO *THE*

Common Noncount Nouns

Count nouns can be counted: *three* dogs, *two* computers, *one* house, *ten* cakes. A noncount noun cannot be counted. Study these commonly used noncount nouns.

Food:	butter	sugar	salt	pepper	soup	rice	fish	meat
	flour	bread						
Liquid:	milk	coffee	water	juice	cream			
Subjects:	English	math	science	music	biology			
Abstract:	love	honesty	poverty	crime	advice	luck	pain	
	hate	beauty	humor					
Others:	homework	information	money	furniture	traffic			

Note:
Noncount nouns use quantifiers such as **much/a little**.*

Examples: We do not have **much** time to finish the assignment.
Can you givew me **a little** water? I am thirsty.

Count nouns use quantifiers such as **many/a few**.*

Examples: There are **many** cars in the parking lot.
Dayna only has **a few** dollars in her wallet.

*See Appendix 11 on page 225 for more information.

Possessive Adjectives

In general, subject pronouns come before the main verb in a sentence. Possessive adjectives come before a noun.

Subject Form	Possessive Adjective Form
I	my
you (singular)	your
he	his
she	her
it	its
we	our
you (plural)	your
they	their

Examples:

I went to Rome last summer with my family.

They like to eat her cooking.

The bird hurt its wing.

Bill called his friends.

APPENDIX 11

Quantifiers

Quantifiers give more information about the quantity, or number, of a noun. Quantifiers usually go in front of a noun. Here are some common examples.

Count	Noncount	Count or Noncount
one, two, three	a little	some (quantity meaning only)
(all numbers)	little	any
a few	much	a lot of
few		the other
many		other
another		
several		
a pair of		
a couple of		

Examples:

Count

<u>Several</u> students went to the school office.

<u>Many</u> people wanted to leave the city.

Elizabeth put <u>a few</u> coins in the parking meter.

Noncount

There is only <u>a little</u> time left before the end of class.

Hurry! We don't have <u>much</u> time.

Count or Noncount

They got into <u>a lot of</u> trouble.

Mrs. Jones has <u>a lot of</u> dogs.

Joanne doesn't have <u>any</u> money.

There aren't <u>any</u> nice houses in this neighborhood.

The Prepositions *At, On,* and *In*

Prepositions express different ideas. They can indicate time, location, and direction. Remember that a preposition is always followed by a noun (or pronoun).

Three very common prepositions in English are *at, on,* and *in.* In general, we use *at* with small, specific times and places, and we use *in* with larger, more general times and places.

	Time	Place
Small:	at 1 P.M.	at McDonald's
Middle:	on Monday	on Princeton Street
Big:	in July	in Orlando
	in spring	in Florida
	in 1995	in the United States
	in this century	in North America

AT

LOCATION

Use *at* for the specific location of an object.

Angela works <u>at</u> the First National Bank.

I always do my homework <u>at</u> my desk.

Jeff met Joanne <u>at</u> the corner of Polk Street and Florida Avenue.

TIME

Use *at* for specific times.

My grammar class meets <u>at</u> 9:00 A.M. every day.

I'll see you <u>at</u> noon for lunch!

Carla doesn't like to walk alone <u>at</u> night.

DIRECTION

Use *at* for motion toward a goal.

>My brother threw a ball <u>at</u> me.

>The robber pointed his gun <u>at</u> the policewoman.

ON

LOCATION

Use *on* when there is contact between two objects. We also use *on* with streets.

>The picture is <u>on</u> the wall.

>He puts his books <u>on</u> the kitchen table.

>Candice lives <u>on</u> Bayshore Boulevard.

TIME

Use *on* with specific days or dates.

>Our soccer game is <u>on</u> Saturday.

>Your dentist appointment is <u>on</u> October 14.

>I was born <u>on</u> June 22, 1968.

IN

LOCATION

Use *in* when something is inside another thing.

>The books are <u>in</u> the big box.

>I left my jacket <u>in</u> your car.

>Barbara lives <u>in</u> Calgary.

TIME

Use *in* for a specific period of time, specific years, or for future appointments.

>I am going to graduate from college <u>in</u> three years.

>My best friend got married <u>in</u> 1994.

>Mr. Johnson always drinks four cups of coffee <u>in</u> the morning.

>We'll meet you <u>in</u> ten minutes.

MORE PREPOSITIONS

Here are a few more common prepositions. Remember that a preposition is usually followed by a noun (or pronoun).

with   to   for   by   near   under   from

Examples:

I am going <u>to</u> France <u>with</u> my cousin.

Marta bought a gift <u>for</u> her grandmother.

Please put that box <u>by</u> the door.

The student union is <u>near</u> my dorm.

Pedro keeps his shoes <u>under</u> his bed.

Did you get a job offer <u>from</u> that company?

Connectors

Coordinating Conjunctions

Coordinating conjunctions are used to connect two independent clauses (sentences).

Note: A comma always appears before a coordinating conjunction that separates two independent clauses.

Purpose	Conjunction	Example
To show reason	**for***	He ate a sandwich, <u>for</u> he was hungry.
To add information	**and**	Carla lives in Toronto, <u>and</u> she is a student.
To add negative information	**nor****	Roberto doesn't like opera, <u>nor</u> does he enjoy hip-hop.
To show contrast	**but**†	The exam was difficult, <u>but</u> everyone passed.
To give a choice	**or**	We can eat Chinese food, <u>or</u> we can order a pizza.
To show concession/contrast	**yet**†	The exam was difficult, <u>yet</u> everyone passed.
To show result	**so**	It was raining, <u>so</u> we decided to stay home last night.

*The conjunction *for* is not common in spoken English.
**Notice question word order is used in the clause that follows *nor*.
†The conjunctions *but* and *yet* have similar meanings. However, *yet* is generally used to show a stronger contrast.

Subordinating Conjunctions

Subordinating conjunctions are used to connect a dependent clause and an independent clause.

Note: When the sentence begins with the dependent clause, a comma should be used after the clause. Following is a list of common subordinating conjunctions.

Purpose	Conjunction	Example
To show reason/cause	**because**	He ate a sandwich <u>because</u> he was hungry.
	since	<u>Since</u> he was hungry, he ate a sandwich.
	as	<u>As</u> he was hungry, he ate a sandwich.
To show contrast	**although**	<u>Although</u> the exam was difficult, everyone passed.
	though	<u>Though</u> the exam was difficult, everyone passed.
	even though	<u>Even though</u> the exam was difficult, everyone passed.
	while	Deborah is a dentist, <u>while</u> John is a doctor.
To show time relationship	**after**	<u>After</u> we ate dinner, we went to a movie.
	before	We ate dinner <u>before</u> we went to a movie.
	until	I won't call you <u>until</u> I finish studying.
	while	<u>While</u> the pasta is cooking, I'll cut the vegetables.
	as	<u>As</u> I was leaving the office, it started to rain.
To show condition	**if**	<u>If</u> it rains tomorrow, we'll stay home.
	even if	We'll go to the park <u>even if</u> it rains tomorrow.

Some Common Comma Rules

1. Put a comma before *and*, *but*, *for*, *or*, *nor*, *so*, *yet*, when they connect two independent clauses.

   Richard bought Julie a candy bar, but he ate it himself.

2. Put a comma between three or more items in a series .

   Jennifer brought a towel, an umbrella, some sunscreen, and a book to the beach.

3. Put a comma after a clause with a connecting word (a dependent clause) when that clause begins a sentence.

   Because it was raining outside, Alex used his umbrella.

4. Put a comma before or after the name of a person spoken to.

   "Hamad, do you want to play soccer?" Ana asked.

   "Do you want to play soccer, Hamad?" Ana asked.

5. Commas separate parts of dates and places. Put a comma between the day and the date. Put a comma between the date and the year. Put a comma between a city and a state or a country.

   I was born on Wednesday, June 27, 1989.

   The concert was in Boston, Massachusetts.

   The headquarters of that company is located in Osaka, Japan.

6. Use a comma to separate an introductory word or phrase from the rest of the sentence.

   Finally, they decided to ask the police for help.

   Every afternoon after school, I go to the library.

7. Put a comma to separate information that is not necessary in a sentence.

   Rome, which is the capital of Italy, has a lot of pollution.

   George Washington, the first president of the United States, was a military officer.

8. Put a comma after the salutation in personal letters and after the conclusion in personal and business letters.

Dear Roberta,	Dear Dr. Smith,	Dear Ms. Kennedy,
Sincerely,	With love,	Yours truly,
Jonathan	Grandma	Alicia

Order of Adjectives

Adjectives can go before nouns.

He has a <u>white</u> car. It is a <u>new</u> car.

When more than one adjective is used before a noun, there is a certain order for the adjectives.

Incorrect: He has a white new car.

Correct: He has a new white car.

In general, there are seven kinds of adjectives, used in this order:

1. size   *small, large, huge*
2. opinion   *beautiful, nice, ugly*
3. shape   *round, square, oval*
4. condition   *broken, damaged, burned*
5. age   *old, young, new*
6. color   *red, white, green*
7. origin   *French, American, Korean*

It is common to have two adjectives before a noun and rare to have three or more adjectives before a noun. When there is more than one adjective before a noun, follow the order above. The noun always goes last. Remember that this list is only a general guideline.

Incorrect: a white small Japanese truck

Correct: a small white Japanese truck

Incorrect: a broken large dish

Correct: a large broken dish

APPENDIX 16

Building Better Sentences

Being a good writer involves many skills: correct grammar, strong vocabulary, and conciseness. Some student writers like to keep their sentences simple. They feel that they will make mistakes writing longer more complicated sentences. However, writing short choppy sentences one after the other is not considered appropriate in academic writing. Study the samples below.

> *The time was yesterday.*
>
> *It was afternoon.*
>
> *A storm approached.*
>
> *It was a strong storm.*
>
> *It was a dangerous storm.*
>
> *The movement of the storm was quick.*
>
> *It moved toward the coast.*
>
> *The coast was in North Carolina.*

Notice that every sentence has an important piece of information. A good writer would not write all these sentences separately. Instead, the most important information from each sentence can be used to create ONE coherent sentence.

Read the sentences again; this time, the important information has been circled.

> The time was (yesterday).
>
> It was (afternoon).
>
> There was a (storm).
>
> The storm was (strong).
>
> The (movement) of the storm was (quick).
>
> It moved towards the (coast).
>
> The coast was in (North Carolina).

234

Here are some strategies for taking the circled information and creating a new sentence.

1. Creating time phrases to begin or end a sentence: *yesterday + afternoon*
2. Finding the key noun: *storm*
3. Finding key adjectives: *strong*

   Creating noun phrases: *a strong + storm*

5. Changing word forms: *movement = move; quick = quickly*

   moved + quickly

6. Creating place phrases: *towards the coast*

   towards the coast (of North Carolina)

   or

   towards the North Carolina coast

Better Sentence:
Yesterday afternoon, a strong storm moved quickly towards the North Carolina coast.

Other strategies for building better sentences include:

- Using connectors and transition words
- Using pronouns as referents for previously mentioned information
- Using possessive adjectives and pronouns

(Susan) (went) somewhere. That place was (the mall). Susan wanted to (buy new shoes). The shoes were for (Susan's mother).

Example:

Susan went to the mall because she wanted to buy new shoes for her mother.

UNIT PRACTICE

This section contains practice for the sentences and paragraphs in Units 1–7. For each practice, read the sentences. Circle the important information in each short sentence. Then write an original sentence from the information you circled. You may want to refer to the list of strategies above. To check your sentence, go to the page and find the sentence in the chapter. Remember, there is more than one way to combine sentences.

Note that the first exercise in Practice 1 has been done for you.

Practice 1

Unit 1: *Understanding Sentence Basics*

A. page 7

1. John is my friend.
2. John works.
3. The work is in Chicago.

My friend John works in Chicago.
_____

B. page 3

1. There are boxes.
2. The boxes are on the table.
3. The boxes are heavy.

_____

_____

C. page 25

1. Caroline attends classes.
2. The classes are at Jefferson Community College.
3. The classes are on Wednesdays.

_____

_____

D. page 29

1. Tuscany is a region.
2. This region is in Italy.
3. This region is beautiful.

_____

_____

Practice 2

Unit 2: Connecting Sentences and Paragraphs

A. page 39

   1. There are books.

   2. The books are rare.

   3. The books are in the library.

_____

_____

B. *Beautiful Snow?*, page 50

   1. Drivers have more accidents.

   2. The accidents happen on roads.

   3. The roads are snowy.

_____

_____

C. *Aspirin*, page 62

   1. Aspirin is good for headaches.

   2. Aspirin is good for colds.

   3. Aspirin is good for pain.

_____

_____

Practice 3

Unit 3: Writing About the Present

A. *Uncle Charlie*, page 69

   1. Charlie is a man.

   2. Charlie is wonderful.

   3. Charlie is my uncle.

_____

_____

B. *My Best Friend*, page 80

    1. Gretchen studies veterinary medicine.

    2. She studies at the University of Florida.

    3. The University of Florida is in Gainesville.

_____

_____

C. page 83 (*Hint:* use a coordinating conjunction here.)

    1. The students take a test.

    2. The test happens every Friday.

    3. There are scores.

    4. The scores are not very high.

_____

_____

Practice 4

Unit 4: *Writing About the Past*

A. *Lao-Tzu and Taoism*, page 95 (*Hint:* use a coordinating conjunction.)

    1. The government was corrupt.

    2. Lao-Tzu decided to leave.

    3. Lao-Tzu left his home.

_____

_____

B. *Moving to the United States*, page 103 (*Hint:* use a coordinating conjunction.)

    1. My parents were not rich.

    2. My parents were always happy.

_____

_____

C. *Muhammad Ibn Batuta,* page 110

    1. This book gives us information.

    2. There is a lot of information.

    3. The book gives us the information now.

    4. The information is important.

    5. The information is about life in the fourteenth century.

_____

_____

Practice 5

Unit 5: *Describing Actions*

A. *A Day Trip for the Johnson Family,* page 115 (*Hint:* use a coordinating conjunction.)

    1. Mr. Johnson loves monkeys.

    2. Rosie loves monkeys.

    3. Mr. Johnson and Rosie are walking to the exhibit.

    4. The exhibit is about monkeys.

_____

_____

B. page 120 (*Hint:* use a coordinating conjunction.)

    1. Bolivia is a country.

    2. Bolivia is landlocked.

    3. Bolivia is in South America.

    4. Switzerland is a country.

    5. Switzerland is landlocked.

    6. Switzerland is in Europe.

_____

_____

C. page 126 (*Hint:* use a coordinating conjunction.)

    1. There are many great places to visit.

    2. These places are in this city.

    3. You can't see all these places.

    4. This can't happen in one day.

_____

_____

Practice 6

Unit 6: *Writing About the Future*

A. Paragraph 54: *Carmen's Fifteenth Birthday*, page 141

    1. First, Carmen arrives.

    2. Then, Carmen will perform some dances.

    3. These dances will be formal.

    4. Carmen is going to do these dances with her friends.

_____

_____

B. page 152

    1. I go to the theater.

    2. The theater is on Broadway.

    3. I do this often.

    4. The reason I do this is that I live in New York.

_____

_____

C. Paragraph 56: *My Winter Vacation*, page 156

    1. First, I will arrive in Canada.

    2. Next, I will buy many souvenirs.

    3. There will be souvenirs for my parents.

    4. There will be souvenirs for my brother.

    5. There will be souvenirs for my friends.

_____

_____

Practice 7

Unit 7: *Writing Sentences with Adjective Clauses and Place Phrases*

A. Paragraph 58: *An Old Family Photo*, page 163

    1. The two women are my mother and grandmother.

    2. The women are sitting on the sofa.

_____

_____

B. Paragraph 61: *Some English Spelling Problems*, page 169

    1. These are words.

    2. There are just a few of these words.

    3. These words cause problems for English speakers.

    4. These speakers are native and nonnative.

_____

_____

C. page 177

    1. Wendy is eating lunch.

    2. Wendy is talking to her friends.

    3. Wendy is in the cafeteria.

    4. Wendy is doing these things right now.

_____

_____

Extra Writing Activities

Read the paragraph and follow the steps below to create a new paragraph. Write the new paragraph on the lines provided. Be sure to write a new title for your paragraph.

EXAMPLE PARAGRAPH

California

[1]California is a large state. [2]It is located in the western part of the United States. [3]The population of California is approximately 34 million. [4]The biggest cities in California are Los Angeles and San Francisco. [5]Millions of tourists visit this state every year. [6]They come for the beaches, the mountains, and the cities that this large state is famous for.

1. In sentences 1, 3, and 4, change *California* to *Florida*. Do the same for the title.

2. In sentence 2, change *western* to *southeastern*.

3. In sentence 3, change the population number from *34 million* to *16 million*.

4. In sentence 4, change the names of the cities from *Los Angeles and San Francisco* to *Miami, Tampa, and Orlando*.

5. In sentence 6, change *mountains* to *parks*.

6. In sentence 6, change *cities* to *great weather*.

_____

_____

_____

_____

_____

_____

_____

_____

| **Writing Activity 2** | **Writing a Paragraph (Unit 2)** |

Read the paragraph and follow the steps below to create a new paragraph. Write the new paragraph on the lines provided. Be sure to write a new title for your paragraph.

My Older Sister

[1]I'd like to tell you about my older sister. [2]Her name is Natalie. [3]She is 26 years old. [4]She is an elementary school teacher. [5]She loves children. [6]She is very patient and kind. [7]My sister Natalie is a wonderful person.

1. In sentences 1 and 7, change *sister* to *brother*. Do the same for the title.

2. In sentences 3, 4, 5, and 6, change *she* to *he*.

3. In sentence 2, change *her* to *his*. Be sure to use a capital letter.

4. Natalie is a girl's name. In sentence 2, change *Natalie* to a boy's name of your choice.

5. In sentence 7, change *wonderful* to *great*.

_____

_____

_____

_____

_____

_____

_____

Writing Activity 3   **Writing a Paragraph (Unit 2)**

Read the paragraph and follow the steps below to create a new paragraph. Write the new paragraph on the lines provided. Be sure to write a new title for your paragraph.

EXAMPLE PARAGRAPH

My House

[1]I live in a big house. [2]It is located on Princeton Street. [3]My house number is 915. [4]My house is new. [5]It is two years old. [6]The sides of my house are light yellow. [7]The roof is light gray. [8]In front of the house, there are many flowers. [9]I am so lucky to live in this house!

1. In sentence 1, change *big* to *little*.

2. In sentence 2, change the name of the street from *Princeton Street* to *Hillside Road*.

3. In sentence 3, change the house number from *915* to *710*.

4. In sentence 4, change *new* to *very old*.

5. In sentence 5, change the number *two* to an appropriate number for a very old house.

6. In sentences 6 and 7, change the color of the side of the house from *light yellow* to *white*. Change the color of the roof from *light gray* to *dark gray*.

7. In sentence 8, change the phrase *many flowers* to *some small bushes and trees*.

_____

_____

_____

_____

_____

_____

_____

Writing Activity 4   **Write a Paragraph (Unit 2)**

Read the paragraph and follow the steps below to create a new paragraph. Write the new paragraph on the lines provided. Be sure to write a new title for your paragraph.

A Desert Plant

EXAMPLE PARAGRAPH

[1]The cactus is an interesting plant. [2]It grows in the desert. [3]It likes very hot temperatures. [4]It does not need a lot of water to live. [5]Its leaves are spiky. [6]Many people grow this plant in their gardens.

1. In sentence 1, change *the cactus* to *seaweed*.
2. In sentence 2, change *desert* to *ocean*. Do the same in the title.
3. In sentence 3, make the verb *likes* negative.
4. In sentence 4, make the verb *does not need* affirmative.
5. In sentence 5, change *spiky* to *long and thin*.
6. In sentence 6, change *gardens* to *aquariums*.

_____

_____

_____

_____

_____

_____

_____

Writing Activity 5 | **Changing Proper Nouns to Subject Pronouns (Unit 2)**

Fill in each blank with the correct subject pronoun (they, she, he, or it) for the proper noun in parentheses ( ). Then copy the new paragraph on the lines below. Give the paragraph a title.

Susan Brown and Joey Chen are actors. (**1.** Joey and Susan) _____ have very

interesting careers. Susan acts in plays in the theater. (**2.** Susan) _____ works in

New York City. (**3.** New York City) _____ is the best place to work in the theater.

Joey acts in movies. (**4.** Joey) _____ works in Los Angeles. (**5.** Los Angeles)

_____ is an exciting city. (**6.** People) _____ make lots of movies there.

Joey and Susan are very happy with their jobs. (**7.** Joey and Susan) _____ would

not do anything else.

_____

_____

_____

_____

_____

_____

_____

_____

_____

Writing Activity 6   Changing Nouns to Object Pronouns (Unit 3)

Read the paragraph and follow the steps below to create a new paragraph. Write the new paragraph on the lines provided. Be sure to write a title for your paragraph.

EXAMPLE PARAGRAPH

¹Last week Jane and I moved into a new apartment. ²We were very excited. ³We moved many big things into (our new apartment). ⁴I had a television. ⁵We put (the television) in the living room next to the window. ⁶Jane's brother helped (Jane and me) move our couch and chairs. ⁷We told (Jane's brother) to put (the couch and chairs) in front of the television. ⁸Finally, we moved in our beds. ⁹It took a long time to bring (the beds) in. ¹⁰Jane said she would move her bed alone, but her brother had to help (Jane). ¹¹Moving is a lot of hard work. I hope we don't have to move again soon!

1. Change all the words in parentheses into an object pronoun (*me, her, him, us, them, it*).

2. In sentence 9, make the verb negative.

3. In sentence 10, change the word *alone* to the phrase *by herself*.

_____

_____

_____

_____

_____

_____

_____

_____

Writing Activity 7   **Past Tense Verbs (Unit 4)**

Read the paragraph and follow the steps below to create a new paragraph. Write the new paragraph on the lines provided.

Life on the Farm

[1]My grandpa is a very busy farmer. [2]Every day he gets up at four o'clock in the morning. [3]He eats breakfast. [4]Then he goes out to the barn. [5]There he feeds and milks the cows. [6]When he finishes, he feeds the rest of the animals. [7]Then he works in the cornfields until noon. [8]He eats a fast lunch. [9]After that, he works in the fields again. [10]In the evening, he eats dinner. [11]Then he feeds the animals one last time. [12]Grandpa finally goes to bed at around nine o'clock. [13]He certainly does a lot in one day!

1. In sentence 2, change *every day* to *yesterday*.
2. In sentences 2–13, change all the verbs to past tense. Be careful of irregular verbs!

Life on the Farm

_____

_____

_____

_____

_____

_____

_____

_____

Writing Activity 8   **Sentence Combining (Unit 4)**

Read the paragraph. It is missing three sentences. Combine the sentences that follow the paragraph. Use and, but, *or* so. *Then write the three new sentences in the correct place in the paragraph.*

Lars's New Career

Lars is studying nursing. (**1.**) _____

_____

_____

Lars also practices nursing at a local hospital. (**2.**) _____

_____

_____

He is not ready to do that yet. (**3.**) _____

_____

_____ Because of this, it will be easy for him to get a

good job. Then he can help as many people as possible.

Missing sentence 1:	He has to go to school five days a week.
	He takes several classes every day.
Missing sentence 2:	He helps with everyday work there.
	He cannot help with emergencies.
Missing sentence 3:	Lars's grades are very good.
	He will graduate with honors.

Writing Activity 9   **Changing Past Tense to Future Tense (Unit 6)**

Read the paragraph and follow the steps below to create a new paragraph. Write the new paragraph on the lines provided.

A Memorable Vacation

¹When I was thirteen years old, my aunt and uncle took me on a wonderful vacation. ²We went to the Black Hills in South Dakota. ³We did lots of interesting things. ⁴We visited Mt. Rushmore and took lots of pictures. ⁵We visited a place to mine for gold. ⁶One night, we even ate buffalo burgers for dinner. ⁷It was very exciting. ⁸I made memories on that trip that I will keep for a lifetime.

1. In sentence 1, change *When I was thirteen years old* to *When I graduate from high school this year.*

2. Change all the verbs in the paragraph to *be going to* + verb.

A Memorable Vacation

Writing Activity 10 | Adjective Clauses (Unit 7)

Read the paragraph below. Three pairs of sentences are underlined. Combine each pair of sentences by using an adjective clause. Rewrite the paragraph with your new sentences on the lines provided. The first pair of sentences has been done for you.

EXAMPLE PARAGRAPH

The Discovery of the *Titanic*

[1]There were many scientists and explorers. They searched for the *Titanic* for a long time. They finally found it in 1985. It was deep in the Atlantic Ocean. This water was too deep for humans to visit without protection. Scientists solved this problem. [2]In order to explore the wreck, they used a **submersible**. This submersible was **controlled** by people on the surface of the ocean. Explorers took pictures of the *Titanic* with the submersible. [3]They even brought things to the surface. These things were on the **sunken** ship. Because of these people's efforts, we now understand more about the remains of the *Titanic*.

submersible: a vehicle that can go very deep underwater

control: to guide

sunken: covered by water

The Discovery of the *Titanic*

There were many scientists and explorers who searched for the *Titanic* for a long time.

_____

_____

_____

_____

_____

_____

APPENDIX

18

Peer Editing Sheets

PEER EDITING SHEET 1   **UNIT 1, Activity 25, page 34**

Writer: _____ Date: _____

Peer editor: _____

1. In three or four words, what is the topic? (What did the writer write about?) _____

   _____

2. How many sentences did the writer write? _____

3. Does each sentence begin with a capital letter? _____ If not, which sentences need to be fixed?

   _____

4. Does each sentence have a period or question mark at the end? _____ If not, which sentences

   need to be fixed? _____

5. What is the longest sentence? _____ How many words does it have? _____

6. Do you see an error in any sentences? If so, write one sentence with a correction here:

   _____

   _____

PEER EDITING SHEET 2   **UNIT 2, Activity 19, page 66**

Writer: _____ Date: _____

Peer editor: _____

1. Where does your partner want to go? _____

2. What is one reason that your partner wants to visit this place? _____

   _____

   _____

3. How many sentences are in your partner's paragraph? _____

4. Did your partner remember to indent the first line of the paragraph? _____

5. Does the paragraph have a topic sentence? _____

6. Write the topic sentence here: _____

   _____

7. Does the paragraph contain any adjectives? If so, write them here. _____

   _____

8. Do you have any questions about what your partner wrote? (Are there any unclear sentences?) If

   so, write your questions here. _____

   _____

   _____

   _____

PEER EDITING SHEET 3   **UNIT 3, Activity 21, page 90**

Writer: _____ Date: _____

Peer editor: _____

1. What sport did the writer choose to write about? _____

2. Did you know about this sport before you read this paragraph? _____

3. Does the paragraph have a topic sentence? _____ If so, write it here. _____

   _____

   _____

4. How many sentences are in the paragraph? _____

5. Does each sentence begin with a capital letter? _____ If not, write the sentences that need to

   be fixed here. _____

   _____

6. Does each sentence have a period or question mark at the end? _____ If not, write the

   sentences that need to be fixed here. _____

   _____

7. Which sentence has the most adjectives in it? Write the sentence here and circle the adjectives.

   _____

   _____

8. Does every sentence have a verb? _____ If not, copy one of the sentences that is missing a

   verb here and add a correct verb. _____

   _____

9. If there is a compound sentence in the paragraph, write it here. Circle the connecting word.

    _____

    _____

10. Did the writer use any object pronouns? If so, write a sentence that contains one here. Circle the

    object pronoun. _____

    _____

11. Write another sentence about the topic here. (Write your own original sentence.)

    _____

    _____

PEER EDITING SHEET 4   **UNIT 4, Activity 18, page 113**

Writer: _____ Date: _____

Peer editor: _____

1. Who did your partner write about? _____

2. Why do you think the writer chose this person? _____

_____

3. Can you find a sentence that tells where the person lived? _____

4. Copy the topic sentence here: _____

_____

_____

5. Now circle the subject in the topic sentence. Underline the verb.

6. How many sentences are there? _____ How many verbs are there? _____

7. In general, it is not good to have the same number of verbs and sentences. If these two numbers

   are the same, this means that the writer uses subject-verb order and simple sentences too often.

   The writer needs to work on sentence variety. Suggest that the writer try to combine sentences.

8. Write a few of the past tense verbs here. _____

9. How many times can you find *was?* _____ *were?* _____ Irregular past verbs? _____

   Past negative verbs? _____

10. Are there any compound sentences that use *but*? _____ If not, suggest two sentences that can be connected with *but*. Write them here.

_____

_____

11. Did the writer use any time phrases? If so, write them here. _____

_____

12. Is there an additional piece of information about the person that you would like to know? Write a question about this information. _____

_____

PEER EDITING SHEET 5   UNIT 5, Activity 15, page 132

Writer: _____   Date: _____

Peer editor: _____

1. Is the first line of the paragraph indented? _____

2. How many *-ing* verbs can you find in the paragraph? _____

3. Can you find a sentence that has *and* or *so* as a connector? Write it here.

   _____

   _____

4. Does every sentence have a subject and a verb? _____ If not, copy one of the incorrect

   sentences here. Then correct it. _____

   _____

   _____

5. Adjectives help make writing easy to see or imagine. Can you find a sentence that does not have any adjectives? Copy it here and add two adjectives. Circle the two adjectives that you added.

   _____

   _____

   _____

6. Does the paragraph have any sentences that contain adverbs of manner? If yes, copy one of them here.

   _____

   _____

   _____

7. Can you find any spelling mistakes? _____ Write the misspelled word and its correct

spelling below.

      Misspelled word   Correctly spelled word

a. _____ a. _____

b. _____ b. _____

c. _____ c. _____

d. _____ d. _____

8. Do you have any comments or suggestions for the writer? If so, write them here.

_____

_____

PEER EDITING SHEET 6   **UNIT 6, Activity 17, page 159**

Writer: _____ Date: _____

Peer editor: _____

1. What event does the writer describe in this paragraph? _____

   _____

   _____

2. Check for these features: a. _____ Is there a topic sentence?

   b. _____ Do all the sentences relate to one topic?

   c. _____ Is the first line indented?

3. What is the topic sentence? Copy it here. _____

   _____

   _____

4. Check for mistakes with subject-verb agreement. If the subject is singular, is the verb singular, too? If the subject is plural, is the verb plural, too? If you find any mistakes, circle them.

5. Is it easy for you to understand the meaning of the sentences in this paragraph? _____

   If not, copy a sentence that is hard for you to understand clearly. _____

   _____

6. Does the writer have articles in every place where they are needed? _____ If not, add

   them in the paper.

7. Do you have any ideas or suggestions for improving the paragraph? _____

   _____

   _____

PEER EDITING SHEET 7   **UNIT 7, Activity 17, page 180**

Writer: _____ Date: _____

Peer editor: _____

1. What is the writer's opinion about cooking food at home or eating in a restaurant? Check one.

    _____ Cooking food at home is better.

    _____ Eating in a restaurant is better.

    _____ Both options are about the same.

2. What is one reason that the writer thinks that choice is better? _____

    _____

3. Copy the sentence here that tells you the answer to number 2. _____

    _____

    _____

4. Does the sentence in number 3 have a subject and a verb? _____ If yes, underline the subject

    one time and the verb two times. If not, add the missing words.

5. Is the first line indented? _____ If not, put an arrow to show that the line needs to be indented.

6. Does the paragraph have a complex sentence? _____ If yes, write it below. If not, make a

    suggestion about combining two simple sentences from the paragraph. _____

    _____

    _____

7. Do you think this paragraph is too long, too short, or just right? _____

8. Does the writer include adjective clauses in the paragraph? Write the clauses below.

_____

_____

9. Do you have any suggestions for making this paragraph better? _____

_____

_____

_____

PEER EDITING SHEET 8   **UNIT 8, Practice 21, page 201**

Writer: _____ Date: _____

Peer editor: _____

1. What is the writer's opinion about smoking in restaurants and bars? _____

   _____

   _____

   _____

2. Do you agree with the writer's opinion? _____

3. Explain your answer in number 2. _____

   _____

   _____

   _____

   _____

4. Check for these features: a. _____ Is there a topic sentence?

   b. _____ Do all the sentences relate to one topic?

   c. _____ Is the first line indented?

5. What is the topic sentence? Copy it here. _____

   _____

   _____

6. Are articles used correctly? Circle any errors with articles.

7. Was it easy for you to understand the language in the paragraph? _____ If not, copy one of the

    confusing parts (sentences) here. _____

    _____

    _____

    _____

8. How many sentences does this paragraph have? _____ How many sentences do *not* have a

    verb? _____

9. Can you think of anything to make this a better paragraph? _____

    _____

    _____

    _____

    _____

PEER EDITING SHEET 9   **UNIT 8, Practice 25, page 205**

Writer: _____ Date: _____

Peer editor: _____

1. What is the writer's opinion about what to do in this case? _____

   _____

   _____

   _____

   _____

2. Do you agree or disagree with the writer's ideas? _____

3. Please explain your answer to number 2. _____

   _____

   _____

   _____

   _____

4. Are all the verbs in the correct tense? If not, write a sentence here with an incorrect verb. Then

   make the correction.

   _____

   _____

5. Does every sentence end in the correct punctuation? _____ If not, put a circle around the

   place where the punctuation should go.

6. Can you understand everything the writer wanted to say? _____ If not, write one of the

unclear parts here. _____

_____

_____

Why is this unclear to you? _____

_____

_____

7. Can you add two or more interesting adjectives in front of two nouns? (Add them on the

student's paper. Draw an arrow to show where they should go.) What are your two adjectives?

Use Appendix 15 if you need help with the correct order. _____

_____

Index